Brimming with creative inspiration, how-to projects, and useful information to enrich your everyday life, Quarto Knows is a favorite destination for those pursuing their interests and passions. Visit our site and dig deeper with our books into your area of interest: Quarto Creates, Quarto Cooks, Quarto Homes, Quarto Lives, Quarto Drives, Quarto Explores, Quarto Gifts, or Quarto Kids.

This edition published in 2019 by Crestline,
an imprint of The Quarto Group
142 West 36th Street, 4th Floor
New York, NY 10018 USA
T (212) 779-4972 F (212) 779-6058
www.QuartoKnows.com

First published in 2014 by Motorbooks, an imprint of Quarto Publishing Group USA Inc., 100 Cummings Center, Suite 265-D, Beverly, MA 01915, USA.

Crestline titles are also available at discount for retail, wholesale, promotional, and bulk purchase. For details, contact the Special Sales Manager by email at specialsales@quarto.com or by mail at The Quarto Group, Attn: Special Sales Manager, 100 Cummings Center Suite 265D, Beverly, MA 01915, USA.

10 9 8 7 6 5 4 3 2

ISBN: 978-0-7858-3750-3

Acquisitions Editor: Darwin Holmstrom
Project Manager: Jordan Wiklund
Art Director: Cindy Samargia Laun
Design and Layout: Karl Laun

On the front cover: 1955 V-8 Roadster
On the back cover: 1968 L88 coupe
On the frontis: detail shot of 1969 L71 Corvette Stingray logo and louvers
On the title page: 1953 Corvette steering column and dashboard (left); 1989 L71 convertible (right)

Printed in Singapore COS072020

CONTENTS

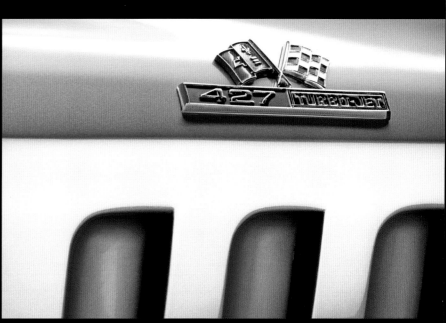

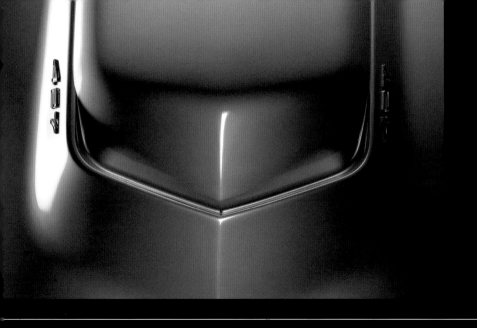

Introduction

The Corvette was one of the first mainstream attempts to bring some of Europe's automotive style and sensibility to the American masses. To accomplish this, it had to look and perform much differently from other American-made automobiles. GM's design chief, Harley Earl, saw to that by basing his introductory version on the British Jaguar XK-120, and then updating it three years later by using the German Mercedes-Benz 300SL as his inspiration. While the first generation Corvette—C1—didn't exactly achieve this goal, it soon became a kind of cultural advertisement for the American way of life: because you live here, you can have this, drive this. The car was not just a vehicle to reach a destination—GM meant it to become a destination in itself. Its styling was startling; its two-seat interior was intimate and exclusive. For Earl, an artist in automobile design, the car's looks were more important than any other feature.

Before World War II, many Americans lived in a vacuum. The nation was large enough that it offered enough to keep us occupied. Artist, painters, and musicians who were dissatisfied with their inspiration at home migrated to Europe, and the very wealthy vacationed there or kept homes there because the change of scenery distracted them from the boredom of their lives. Most of America's population had fled other countries, and they frequently abandoned their heritage as well. War exposed 16 million Americans to vast amounts of new stimuli. Many of these soldiers were second- and third-generation Americans with no firsthand memories of their homelands. For them, it may have felt as if they had landed on the moon. As they landed in Morocco in 1942, Britain in 1943, and France, Italy, Germany, and Russia in 1944 and 1945, even the most reluctant of them were force-fed cultural differences in unfamiliar ideas, concepts, food, dress, housing, priorities, and values.

Until this time, the idea that a major U.S. automaker might market a lightweight two-seater was unthinkable, and perhaps unnecessary. Other parts of the world required agile economical motor vehicles where governments taxed gasoline much higher than in the United States, and where the paved roads followed natural geographic features, circuitous historic cow paths, or simply wove through narrow lanes in tightly congested cities.

In contrast to this, early in the history of the United States, our congress enacted the Northwest Territory Act of 1787. This ordinance laid out what became the American Midwest, and it set the pattern for our roads. Wisconsin, Illinois, Indiana, Ohio, and Michigan were sectioned in precise one-mile grids with roads set arrow-straight along the major compass headings. By the middle of the twentieth century, with dirt cheap gas and roads that barely swerved from horizon to horizon, maneuverability in an American car was extraneous.

But the consciousness raising that took place in the minds of millions of G.I.s who went abroad, and to their spouses who labored in materiel production factories during the war, brought profound changes in attitudes. The unthinkable now was possible, and what was *different* became necessary, especially from an organization seeking total control of all the markets for each of its ideas. This was a corporation that already marketed 80 kinds of cars, and didn't think 81 were too many. The Corvette was born into this environment.

Through its 60-plus years on the market, the Corvette has come to represent a kind of allegory for the changes that occurred in postwar America. When the car appeared at Motorama, GM's traveling showcase event, Earl and his design staff had imprinted it with the logos of a technologically oriented world poised on the brink of the space age. GM reinforced this message not only with the space age material with which it manufactured the car, but also in the rocket contrail-like taillights, and the name of the original engine—the "Blue Flame Special."

From its conception, the Corvette was about its looks and how they dictated taste and inspired desire. It had to do all the things other cars did—accelerate and turn and stop—but its inventor, Harley Earl, was more interested in turning heads and stopping people in their tracks. His talented designers and their successors created the series of automobiles that has, through its lines and shapes, defined and exemplified the American sports car from 1953 through the present day. It is those lines and shapes that we examine and admire here.

HARLEY EARL'S CHOICE OF PLASTIC as a building material reflected a postwar decision-making mentality based on wartime self-sufficiency and practicality. The U.S. Office of Wage and Price Controls had limited the rewards that businesses and their laborers received throughout the war. Within weeks after the Japanese surrender in September 1945, more than 100,000 workers lost their jobs as the War Department cancelled equipment production contracts. Those still employed were frustrated by hard work but unchanged wages, and 43,000 oil workers almost immediately went on strike against petroleum producers. Chrysler's labor force, disappointed by the salary increase offered them, walked off the production line at the number three automaker and stayed out for 100 days. When they settled, Henry Ford locked out 50,000 of his workers who demanded a similar pay raise. In similar labor actions against GM, more than 225,000 autoworkers walked out on the carmakers. The same desire for fairer wages put 750,000 steel workers and steelmakers at odds in January 1946, forcing a presidential intervention to keep the mills open. While the owners and the steel workers reached agreement in 1951, automakers had begun looking for other fabricating materials that relied less on what they saw as an industry driven by self-centered greed on both sides of the negotiating table. When a research chemist introduced GM executives to a prototype car bodied in fiberglass, Harley Earl saw nothing but opportunity.

The Corvette came to symbolize a Future-rama society that politicians and corporate leaders wanted to project to the world. Not only was this philosophy

to offer "a car for every purse and purpose," as GM's chairman Alfred Sloan famously expressed in the late 1940s, but the glamorous life itself was *also* available in the United States, open all to those who sought it. Shiploads of immigrants arrived after the war to help build and to earn their chance at living the American dream. While the car's six-cylinder engine and two-speed automatic transmission frustrated some of Chevrolet's enthusiast engineers and earned it scorn from a few sports car snobs, these individuals never were the audience for whom the car was intended. General Motors publicly excused its severely limited product launch, held to just 300 units, as their corporate attention to production details. But just as surely, GM calculated the exclusivity of this striking automobile to emphasize how some politicians and corporate chieftains wanted those who were not going to get a new Corvette to see the future in America: maybe not yours, even if you seek it.

The first generation Corvette, C1, may have been compromised at birth by time, budget limitations, and by GM's need to interpret and translate a foreign concept. But Chevrolet engineers and stylists steadily transformed the C1, not because they wanted it to be the European car of our dreams in America, but because it's in our nature to bring something into our culture and to change it and make it our own. It is an American trait to believe that we can improve everything, and Corvette's second generation models, the sleek, sexy C2 Stingray coupe and convertible, proved the theory: we are exceptional, and everything we produce must be as well.

1 1953 CORVETTE

It took nearly a year and a half of behind-the-scenes machinations and manipulations by General Motors' most powerful decision makers. The Chevrolet Corvette had been an idea shared by Vice President of Styling Harley Earl, Chevrolet General Manager Tom Keating, Chevy's chief engineer Ed Cole, GM's president Harlow Curtice, and board chairman Alfred Sloane. Each of these men had their own methods of taking the pulse of the auto-buying public, but all their theories came together in the wide, low, handsomely styled two-seater. Fulfilling their promise to anxious customers and watchful media, they began production on June 30, 1953.

PROUD OF THEIR CONCEPT for this American sports car, but well aware of the challenges of introducing it in a hurry, GM settled on a modest first-year production of just 300 copies. Assemblers were working with an unfamiliar body material—fiberglass—and the outside suppliers suffered growing pains as they got their processes going for the new fiberglass-bodied sports car.

GM had introduced the car at its recently launched Motorama traveling auto shows, and public response was wildly enthusiastic. Hundreds of potential customers—many more than the 300 GM planned to satisfy—had told exhibit personnel and their own dealers that they were ready to buy. Chevrolet management intended the production limit to promote the desirability and exclusivity of the new convertible.

GM's chief of research and development, Maurice Olley, devised a simple chassis that used parts from other Chevrolet models. As development progressed, this "borrowed" inventory grew to include the Corvette's inline, six-cylinder engine and two-speed automatic transmission. These last two elements were compromises because none of GM's divisions, each with their own V-8 engines, were willing to share. Ed Cole, who had been Cadillac's chief engineer before his promotion to the larger Chevrolet division, imported his engine specialist, Harry Barr, and the two of them supervised efforts to increase the Chevy six from 115 horsepower to 150, giving the Corvette a top speed of 108 miles per hour and acceleration from 0–60 miles per hour in 11 seconds.

Chevrolet had nearly 7,600 dealers across North America, and *all* of them wanted a Corvette. General Sales Manager William Fish finally allocated cars to only the division's largest-volume outlets with the highest-visibility regular customers. By late September 1953, Chevrolet had delivered the first 50 cars to just such owners. As of year-end, 183 were in private hands. The rest became engineering tests, dealer display models, and perks for GM executives, or entered the pool for national auto shows.

Chevrolet's strategy was not entirely successful. The Corvette, conceived as an $1,800 automobile, came in at $3,490, approaching the price of an entry Cadillac but without the luxury brand's roll-up windows, tight-fitting top, and other creature comforts. Some of those celebrity buyers Chevrolet had hoped would love the car and tell their friends were disappointed, but they told their friends anyway.

Chevrolet assembled the 1953 models in a small facility in Flint, Michigan, a structure so small that 300 cars pushed its capacity. They planned to move production to St. Louis for 1954 where they targeted manufacture at 1,000 cars a month. That proved wildly optimistic.

2

1955 V-8 ROADSTER

With St. Louis geared up to assemble 1,000 Corvettes each month, manufacturing found it had to slam on the brakes.

THE POTENTIAL BUYERS who had rapturously proclaimed to Motorama staff and dealer salespeople their desire to buy a Corvette (at $1,800) felt betrayed by its higher price, the Bowtie division's arrogance, and more importantly by the car's disappointing performance and quality. Production totaled only 3,939 cars between June 30, 1953, and December 31, 1954. But St. Louis began the 1955 calendar year with 1,076 cars on hand because Chevrolet had sold only 2,863 of that total. Board members urged Alfred Sloan to kill the car and write off the losses. But that was not Sloan's philosophy. He and his chief financial advisor, Donaldson Brown, hewed to their belief that products must find their market and a corporation must wait for its return on investment.

That helped save the Corvette from premature extinction. But other factors—some far out of GM's control—aided and abetted Sloan's strategy. In late 1952, Ford Motor Company learned of Chevrolet's planned sports car. A former GM stylist named Franklin Hershey headed Ford's design department, and overnight he launched an around-the-clock effort to produce a competitive model. Early in January 1953, as Chevy's concept wowed first-time viewers in the Motorama shows, Hershey gained approval from Henry Ford II to proceed to production with his department's concept for the 1955 Thunderbird.

The second factor that breathed new life into the Corvette came internally. Ed Cole accelerated the Chevrolet division's plans to introduce its own V-8 engine. Cole set Harry Barr to work. Barr revised and improved the existing plan, making the 265–cubic inch engine into a 195-horsepower option for 1955 production. Barr and his engineers beefed up the two-speed Powerglide automatic, and they added a manual, three-speed transmission to the Corvette inventory.

During this time an outspoken outsider approached Chevrolet and asked for a job. Zora Arkus-Duntov had seen the car at the Motorama debut in the Waldof-Astoria hotel and, as a racer and engineer, believed he could improve it. He wrote to Cole, presenting his credentials and his ideas. His letter showed he had valuable insight into the car's potential—not only from a performance standpoint, but also from perspectives of image and marketing. Chevrolet hired him and assigned him to assist research and development head Maurice Olley.

For 1954, Chevrolet styling had introduced three new colors to enliven the appeal of the Polo White convertible: Pennant Blue, Sportsman Red, and black. But ambitious plans for a "facelift" for 1955 went the way of even more costly proposals to convert the fiberglass body to steel. The car provoked head scratching and soul searching even within Chevrolet division. Chief engineer Ed Cole admitted years later to historian Karl Ludvigsen that at the time "we had no real feeling for the market. Was the Corvette for the boulevard driver or the sports-car tiger?"

Ironically it was Ford's Thunderbird—as the V-8 engine, electric window–equipped boulevard cruiser—that helped define the Corvette's place. Sales figures by year-end 1955 delivered the verdict. Ford had sold more than 16,000 of its powerful, plush T-Birds, while St. Louis had manufactured just 700 Corvettes, and only 693 of them left St. Louis with the new V-8. Fortunately, Alfred Sloan was still in charge, along with his patient attitude.

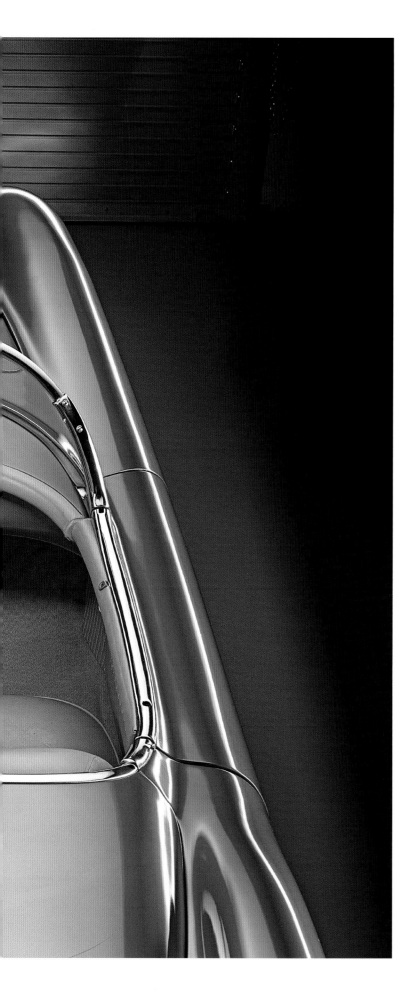

TIGER!

A Corvette is no tame kitten.

Sure, it can purr softly and gently as any household tabby, idling along in the sun. But even so, you catch a hint — a certain lithe competence in the way it moves, an undertone of raw power in the velvety exhaust.

For this one is a tiger! Under its sleek hood beats a savage heart — the steel-sheathed fury of 195 V8 horsepower. Its broad tread clings to the road with an incredible footsureness. And its 16-to-1 steering ratio, the taloned grip of its huge brakes, give it lightning-fast reflexes.

It is a tiger — but an obedient tiger. This fury of acceleration, these whiplash reflexes, are servant to the slightest nudge of your foot, the fractional pressure of your fingers. Your eye and your nerves command these steel muscles with an absoluteness you have never even dreamed.

True, this car can slip through the tangle of traffic with effortless serenity, its special Powerglide transmission metering out a faultless flow of power. In its foam-rubber seats, its deep floor-carpeting, its glove-soft upholstery, are the true marks of luxury.

But the tiger is always there . . . just under the surface. And, if there is fire in your blood . . . if your heart soars to the harsh music of excitement . . . this is the car that was meant for you. Corvette is its name. And *action* is its business. . . . Chevrolet Division of General Motors, Detroit 2, Michigan.

CHEVROLET CORVETTE

29

3

1957
Fuel-Injected V-8
CONVERTIBLE

"Fuel-injection saved the Corvette," Ken Kayser said, "because it made the car exotic." Kayser would know.

AS AUTHOR OF THE DEFINITIVE and fascinating *History of GM's Ramjet Fuel Injection on the Chevrolet V-8 and Its Corvette Racing Pedigree*, he recognized that this high-tech mechanical fuel delivery system put the road-going Corvette on a par with the German-made Mercedes-Benz 300SL models that cost twice as much. Mercedes' racing cars introduced it in 1955, and now America's car for the boulevard driver and the sports-car tiger offered the same sophistication.

Fuel injection symbolized other changes within Chevrolet and for the Corvette. GM promoted Ed Cole to the job of Chevrolet division manager, and Cole elevated Harry Barr to the job of division chief engineer. Barr's engineering staff increased the 265 V-8 displacement to a soon-to-be legendary 283 cubic inches by enlarging cylinder bore 0.125 inches. With carburetors, engine output ranged upward from 220 horsepower all the way to 270 with twin four-barrel units. And with Rochester's fuel injection, the Corvette delivered 250 or 283 horsepower, reaching the mythical goal of one horsepower output per cubic inch of displacement

For the 1956 model year, Chevrolet had introduced the redesigned Corvette body. While Jaguar's XK-120 had been Harley Earl's benchmark for the 1953 Corvette, adopting its wheelbase and engine configuration, Mercedes' 300SL roadster became a visual inspiration for the '56 Corvette. Gone were the troublesome side curtains that owners of 1953, '54, and '55 models had to contend with in rain or cold. Roll-up glass windows replaced the finicky plastic predecessors, and customers found an option for electric window lifts on order sheets. Harley Earl's stylists introduced the recessed side "cove" as a design element that broke up the slab sides of the first cars and offered opportunities for introducing two-tone paint schemes. To the original white, red, blue, and black colors available in 1955, Chevy added Aztek Copper and Cascade Green. After the dismal 700-unit production of 1955, the redesigned car began to find its audience, and St. Louis turned out 2,934 through the 1956 model year.

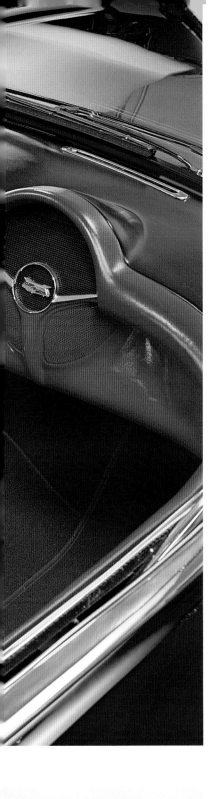

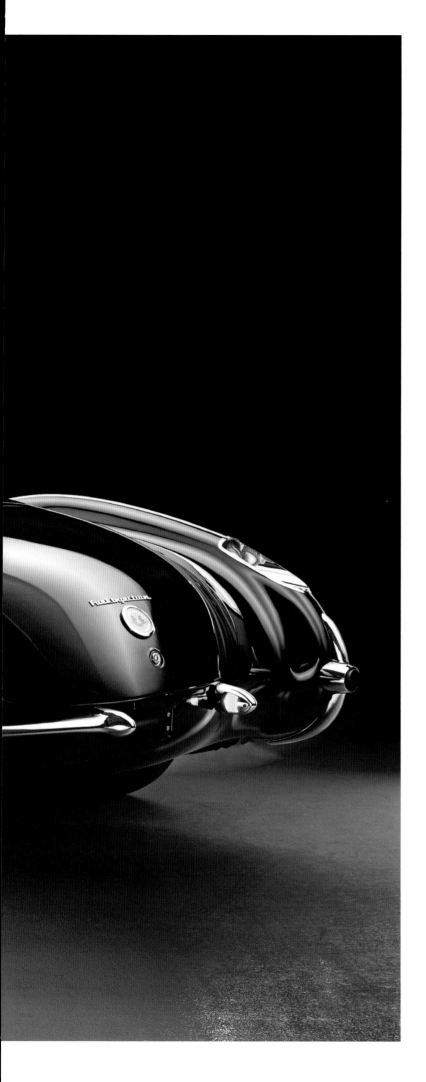

"REALLY, OLD BOY, YOU AREN'T SUPPOSED TO BUILD THAT SORT OF THING IN AMERICA, Y'KNOW."

The unforgivable thing, of course, is this: The new Corvette not only looks delightful and rides like the Blue Train—but it also is quite capable of macerating the competition out on the road circuits.

This dual nature is the classic requirement before you can call a pretty two-seater a *sports car*. And properly so, for this is an honorable name, and only a vehicle with race-bred precision of handling, cornering and control can make a mortal driver feel quite so akin to the gods.

Unlike the gentleman above, who has been a little slow in catching up with current events, most sports car people are becoming aware that the Corvette is truly one of the world's most remarkable cars. Because it does two disparate things outstandingly well: It provides superbly practical motoring, with every luxury and convenience your heart might covet, and accompanies this with a soul-satisfying ferocity of performance.

We could recite the full specifications. But if you are the kind of driver who is meant for a Corvette, you'll want to find out firsthand—and that, sir, would be our pleasure! . . . *Chevrolet Division of General Motors, Detroit 2, Michigan.*

SPECIFICATIONS: *283-cubic-inch V8 engine with single four-barrel carburetor, 220 h.p. (four other engines* range to 283 h.p. with fuel injection). Close-ratio three-speed manual transmission standard, with special Powerglide automatic drive* available on all but maximum-performance engines. Choice of removable hard top or power-operated fabric top, Power-Lift windows.* Instruments include 6000 r.p.m. tachometer, oil pressure gauge and ammeter.   *Optional at extra cost.*

by Chevrolet

The Rochester fuel-injection system arrived at the same time Corvettes introduced their four-speed, manual transmission. This $188-option appealed to 664 buyers, slightly more than 10 percent of the total 6,339 production. Fuel injection went out on 1,040 cars.

Following early efforts and a few successes at racing the Corvettes, Chevrolet introduced several options directly aimed at competition customers, including a heavy-duty racing suspension and a boxy fresh-air intake system for the engine and for brake cooling. These upgrades were a delicate matter because General Motors' chairman Frederick Donner had co-signed an agreement with the other domestic automakers to not participate in or promote racing as a safety gesture to fend off potential US government regulations that might have restricted performance, engine output, or other independent decisions.

4

1959
Fuel-Injected V-8
4-SPEED CONVERTIBLE

After introducing a new body style for 1956, Chevrolet updated Corvette styling again just two years later for 1958, introducing quad headlights and a great deal of decorative trim that included non-functional hood louvers and twin chrome spears that hugged the contours of the rear deck lid. Production surged nearly 45 percent from 6,339 in 1957 to 9,168 for 1958.

THE 1958 MODEL YEAR marked the end of Harley Earl's long, influential, and successful career with GM, and his tenure, especially through the 1950s, was probably best known for its barely restrained excesses. His successor, Bill Mitchell—while perhaps even more flamboyant in his person than Earl was—quickly removed elements of the Earl legacy from GM's cars. For 1959, both the front louvers and rear deck chrome disappeared.

'59 CORVETTE

by Chevrolet

ONCE AGAIN, THE REAL McCOY—WITH AN EVEN SWEETER, SOLIDER WAY OF GOING!

Here's the '59 version of America's only honest-to-Pete sports car. The changes are not earth-shaking when you read them—but wait until you drive this one. Try the new parallelogram rear suspension and see what it does to power hop—how it nails all that torque right down on the pavement, how it smoothes the rear-end steering effect, how it cuts axle wind-up under hard braking. Check the new form-fitting seats, the reverse lockout in the four-speed transmission*, the new "road" version of our metallic-lined brakes*, the subtle improvements in driving position, the easier-to-read instruments.

But you get the idea. The '59 has been honed and polished and refined. And we feel free to say now that this is not only a veritable sports car—but it will handle, go and hang on better than any other production sports car in the world. Bar none!

It is a pure delight to drive. And if you haven't given Corvette a chance to talk to you yet, don't put it off any longer. This is the real thing, for real drivers. . . . Chevrolet Division of General Motors, Detroit 2, Michigan.

*extra-cost option

The new models carried over engines and transmission configurations virtually unchanged, and engine outputs were identical to 1958 numbers. Carbureted engines offered 230 horsepower and optional versions produced 245 and 270 horsepower with dual four-barrels. Fuel-injected engines delivered 250 and 290 horsepower. Buyers voted with their pocket books for the standard three-speed transmission, or the optional Powerglide or four-speed manual gearbox. In all, 7,792 buyers out of the 9,670 production run of 1959 models preferred to shift themselves with the split between three- and four-speeds almost equal. A total of 4,175 buyers felt the four-speed was worth the additional $188.30. (Chevy had reduced its price from $215.20 for 1958.)

Chassis improvements—some derived from outside racing work—added trailing radius rods to the rear suspension. This so-called "parallelogram" suspension linked the top of the rear axle to the rear edge of the frame. It resisted the rear axle's tendency to twist in hard acceleration.

The 1958/1959 model years represented the validation of Alfred Sloan's belief in giving a car time to find its market. The Corvette turned a profit for Chevrolet division and General Motors late in 1958. By this time, Bill Mitchell had his stylists working on an all-new 1961 model, inspired by vehicles he had seen at European auto shows and in foreign automobile magazines. Mitchell and his Chevrolet staff had created a series of show cars that—unknown to viewers at the time—revealed many of the forms and much of the style of the next Corvette. But Chevrolet had other products to update, and these each sold many more units than the Corvette did. For the second time in its young life, management delayed updating the styling of the sports car.

Sting Ray
Z06 COUPE

A glance at the all-revealing "build sheet" for this coupe shows off some options that were not possible for mere mortal customers to obtain. But the intended driver of this car had inside information, and he also had clout. Much of the inside information came from inside his own brain—this car was Zora Duntov's Z06 development mule. And along with the Z06's obligatory 36-gallon fuel tank—the so-called "big tank"—Zora's car came with air conditioning.

AS STING RAY CO-DESIGNER PETER BROCK EXPLAINED in his excellent and insightful 2013 book, *Corvette Stingray*, Harley Earl and Bill Mitchell each had a vision for what Corvette's second generation model should be. As early as 1955, Earl had his "fellahs" (as he called his stylists) working on the new car. But poor sales and indifferent (at best) support of the Corvette among GM's higher management swept his concepts out of contention. Earl still believed in the Corvette's market and performance potential, though, so as he prepared for retirement he pushed through a Corvette SS racing project that had lasting effects on the vehicle. But the hastily developed SS suffered several indignities at Sebring in early 1957, and, with the instigation of the racing ban, the SS disappeared into storage. The mantle of perpetuating Corvette styling fell on Earl's successor, Bill Mitchell, and he wasted no time making it his own. After returning from the Turin Auto Show in Italy, he showed a pile of his own photos of show cars and speed-record contenders to a group of designers in one of his research studios. Brock was there, and he recalled the assignment in *Corvette Stingray*: "I want this form to be a complete breakaway from what we've seen around here in the past," Mitchell told the group. That included, as Brock remembered, "NO MORE FINS."

While Brock and his colleagues sketched hundreds of concepts, Zora Duntov and his engineers worked on a new chassis that incorporated the 327–cubic inch V-8 introduced for 1962, but now connected to the road through Chevrolet's first independent rear suspension. To fit the system under the car's stylish rear end dictated the use of a transverse-mounted rear spring, a clever adaptation that fit the package and gave the car greatly improved handling. Duntov had innovated a rear-mounted transmission, a transaxle assembly that would have further improved handling through better weight balance. But space and cost considerations sidelined the transaxle.

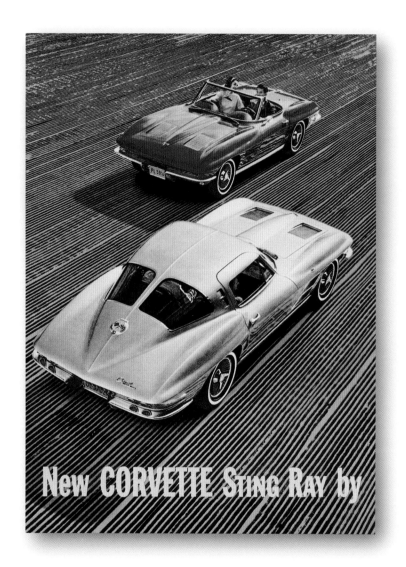

One of the car's most distinctive design features excited Mitchell, engaged Brock, but enraged Duntov. Mitchell had long admired the prominent center spine on Jean Bugatti's 1935 Type 57 fastback prototype. The car, fabricated in Elektron—a delicate and difficult-to-work magnesium alloy—incorporated a folded seam to join the vast roof panels using rivets. Mitchell wanted a milder variation of that he referred to as a "windsplit." When Duntov saw it, he was disappointed, arguing that it would make rear visibility very difficult. A day later, after a shouting match with Mitchell, Duntov was discouraged. The "split window" survived, but only for the first year. Duntov was right, but Mitchell had made it clear that he and his stylists exerted far more influence on upper management than the single outspoken engineer did.

6

Modified
STING RAY COUPE

It's often the case that a great story has an element of "on the one hand . . . while on the other hand . . ." The history of this 1966 L72 coupe is just such an example.

IT BEGAN IN 1966, when the original purchaser of this car ordered it for his teenage son. Out of 22,720 Corvettes that the St. Louis plant assembled during that model year, this was number 6,712, and it left the assembly line on March 16, 1966.

The buyer, a wealthy resident of Beverly Hills, California, optioned it the way any son of such a man could wish: J56 heavy-duty brakes; G81 Posi-Traction rear differential; P48 "Quick Take-Off Wheels"; L72 427–cubic inch, 425-horse-power turbo-jet V-8; M22 4-speed, close-ratio, heavy-duty transmission; and the legendary Muncie "Rock Crusher" gearbox. To reinforce the sense that there was nothing sub-tle about this order, he selected paint code 974: Rally Red. Imagine Marilyn Monroe's lipstick, with a hint of orange, be-ginning to melt in the sun on a hot Beverly Hills afternoon.

It's a safe bet the generous dad suspected his son really was going to drive the car hard, so the stronger transmission was a prudent choice. He also gave his son leather seats, tinted glass, and the AM/FM radio. The options fees came to $1,632.70, and with destination charges, the window sticker totaled $6,039.45.

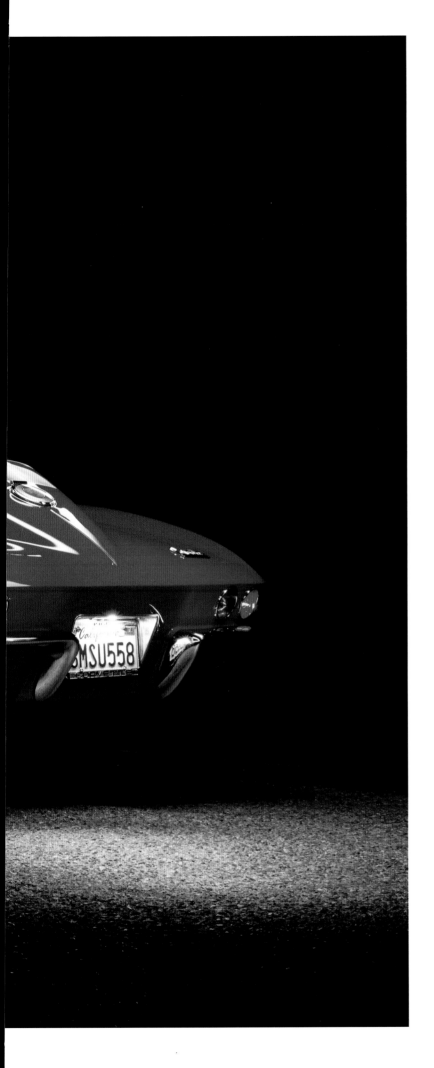

It's not surprising to learn that the dad's expectations came true: the young man blew up the engine just a few months after taking delivery. The Beverly Hills dealer—Emerald Chevrolet, at 350 North Canon Drive—examined the V-8 and ordered a replacement. You can't help but read this and think, "It must have been pretty good to be that fortunate son." Well, yes, on the one hand it was.

On the other hand, shortly after Emerald replaced the engine, the young man received his draft notice. After basic training he was sent to Vietnam, and in 1968, he was killed in action.

His family, especially his father, was devastated. The young man's parents parked the coupe in the garage and left it. For almost 30 years, until the father died in 1997, the car sat untouched, undriven, unpreserved. At the estate sale following the father's death, a southern California auto restorer and parts vendor bought the car, got it running, and restored the interior and exterior. Nearly a year later, in mid-1998, the current owner acquired the car at an auction.

Deciding he wanted a car to drive more than one to admire in the garage, he embarked on a mechanical restoration, overhauling the engine, transmission, front and rear axles, and rear trailing arms. He did all this himself, along with replacing all the wiring. He restored the retractable headlight motors, something he described as "quite a challenging effort" because for hours he stood folded over, looking upside down into the headlight cavities.

The restorer came by his skills naturally. He had bought his first car when he was in the eighth grade, sharing the five-dollar cost of a clapped-out Willys with his best friend. They turned that car into a successful B-gas dragster. For one of his early jobs, he painted cars and body panels for the fiberglass manufacturer that molded Corvette bodies. Some 43 cars later, perhaps with a memory in mind, he bought the Corvette.

He upgraded the engine electronics to improve drivability and performance, adding a Petronic Electronic Ignition and an MSD racing ignition system. To this ongoing evolution, he updated to a modern AM/FM sound system, a new Holly Street Avenger carburetor, and larger wheels and radial tires on a new, stiffer racing suspension. He replaced the radiator, a change he described as essential to enjoy the car and protect the engine during the six years he lived in Arizona. He added the 1967 "stinger" front deck lid because its air scoop opens to feed the 427 with sufficient cold air. Recognizing the fact that, should he ever sell the car, its next owner may have a different perspective on its use and appearance, he kept all the original parts to restore the car to its 1966 configuration. He hints that it would take a truck to haul away all those parts, but that will not be happening any time soon.

The L72 engine presents a curious element to this story. Almost from the start of the automobile, engine designers sought to improve performance and increase power output. For decades, it seemed impossible for an engine ever to produce as much as one horsepower per cubic inch, let alone putting out more than that. Then, in 1957, Chevrolet's engineers offered their 283–cubic inch V-8 with 283 horsepower. They had crossed the Rubicon and there was no looking back. A year later, 283 cubes produced 290 horses, and in 1960, one version developed 315. The much-admired 327 V-8 offered as much as 360 horsepower with fuel injection in 1962 and 1963, increasing to 375 for 1964. In 1965, a new legend arrived on the Corvette platform—the 396–cubic inch V-8, which boasted 425 horsepower. It was no empty boast, however, and this powerplant and Corvette model opened the floodgates; other manufacturers introduced "big-block" displacement to road-going customers. Model year 1966 became hallowed in performance-car history as the moment Chevrolet brought out its 427 for the Corvette. Curiously, however, the Bowtie management rated its peak output at 450 horsepower, but midyear dropped the figure to 425, the same as the previous year's 396.

Corvette Sting Ray Sport Coupe with eight standard safety features, including outside rearview mirror. Use it always before passing.

The day she flew the coupe

What manner of woman is this, you ask, who stands in the midst of a mountain stream eating a peach?

Actually she's a normal everyday girl except that she and her husband own the Corvette Coupe in the background. (He's at work right now, wondering where he misplaced his car keys.)

The temptation, you see, was over-powering. They'd had the car a whole week now, and not once had he offered to let her drive. His excuse was that this, uh, was a big hairy sports car. Too much for a woman to handle: the trigger-quick steering, the independent rear suspension, the disc brakes—plus the 4-speed transmission and that 425-hp engine they had ordered—egad! He would

teach her to drive it some weekend. So he said.

That's why she hid the keys, forcing him to seek public transportation. Sure of his departure, she went to the garage, started the Corvette, and was off for the hills, soon upshifting and downshifting as smoothly as he. His car. Hard to drive. What propaganda!

'66 CORVETTE BY CHEVROLET

Chevrolet Division of General Motors, Detroit, Michigan

63

This was not a typo, nor did it represent detuning. On the one hand, engineering staff conservatively had rated its output at 450 horsepower. Unmuffled aluminum-block 427s had topped 550 horsepower on GM's dynos. On the other hand, with insurance companies already tired of paying claims on crashes and thefts of these high-performance models, All-State Insurance led the industry in alerting manufacturers and policyholders that after midyear 1966, it no longer would cover automobiles whose rated power exceeded engine displacement. Auto insurance company lobbyists with deep pockets already had caught the attention of legislators in Congress. Some of the early 1966 models escaped St. Louis with a sticker proclaiming 427/450 horsepower, but that nomenclature changed when the insurance industry lined up against high output.

7

1966
STING RAY L72
Convertible

General Motors had imposed a rule on all its divisions that restricted the largest displacement engines to be used only in the full-size models.

GM'S BOARD HOPED THAT THIS STRATEGY made the corporation appear conscientious to Washington lawmakers. Early in 1965, however, division product planners who had monitored their competitors and the rapidly growing interest in high performance worked up sales projections for other models with these potent engines. Chairman Frederick Donner, who had pushed through the racing ban effectively in 1957, was neither a designer nor an engineer, but he was a numbers man, and the sales potential of big displacement and high horsepower spoke to him. He rescinded the ban starting with the 1966 model year.

Corvette and other Chevrolet product planners quickly inserted 427–cubic inch displacement V-8s onto the option sheets. The base engine for Corvettes had been the 327–cubic inch block since 1963. Back then, it developed 250 horsepower, and the most aggressively tuned version with fuel injection produced 360 horsepower from the same engine. That output peaked at 375 for 1964 and 1965. The 396–cubic inch L72 appeared that year, skirting Donner's previous limits as it put out 425 horsepower.

Model year 1966 changed things around. Fuel injection disappeared, and all engines used Holley carburetors for fuel delivery. The 427–cubic inch displacement appeared in two versions on option sheets: the L36, with 390 horsepower, at $181.20; and the 425-horsepower L72, at $312.85. These engines sat under the so-called "bubble" hood that Chevrolet had introduced on the 1965 396–cubic inch models. Production numbers of the two engines were nearly identical, with 5,116 of the 390 and 5,258 of the 425 manufactured. With the coupe introduction in 1963, the combined assembly total of Sting Ray coupes and convertibles cracked 20,000 vehicles, settling at 21,513 cars. This figure climbed steadily to reach 27,720 for 1966. Four-speed manual transmissions outnumbered the three-speed Powerglide by nearly ten to one, with only 2,401 customers preferring the automatic while 24,755 cars emerged from St. Louis with either the M20 wide-ratio manual, M21 close-ratio, or the M22 heavy-duty close-ratio gearbox. Sports-car tigers were leading the efforts to define the car.

The Chevrolet built for two.

It started, that morning, with hints. Work-weary, he says. Kid-frazzled, she says. Who gets the Corvette today? You do. No, you do. Ah. *We do.*

So. Arrangements made. Hamper stocked and stowed in the Corvette. No room for people back there. A

pity. But you don't compromise so much as an inch when you build America's only true production sports car. Which is why it comes with four-wheel disc brakes, thread-needle steering and fully independent suspension.

Now. He rouses Corvette's Turbo-

Jet V8, the 390-hp version they'd chosen as tractable enough for her and satisfying enough for him. Then, away. Outside the city unwinds a road as long as the day ahead. A day just for them. In the Chevrolet built just for two.

'66 CORVETTE BY CHEVROLET

Bill Mitchell's stylists and Zora Duntov's engineers had begun working on the next generation Corvette as soon as the 1963 Sting Ray appeared.

THE DISTANT HORIZON SHOWED automakers the dawn of a new day of vehicle safety and engine emissions legislation; product development accomplished in only 24 months in the 1950s stretched to 36 and longer by the mid-1960s. Savvy enthusiasts and journalists working for automotive magazines heard rumors during 1965 that the next Corvette was due for 1967. With Chevrolet's new Camaro requiring more work and more personnel to address lingering glitches, the division moved the introduction back one more year.

What emerged for 1967 was the cleanest of the Sting Ray bodies. Where the 1963 introductory cars sported mock air inlets and engine deck lid grilles, by its final year, the second generation Corvette, the C2, emerged as the least decorated Vette to date. What also emerged were the most powerful road-going engines yet.

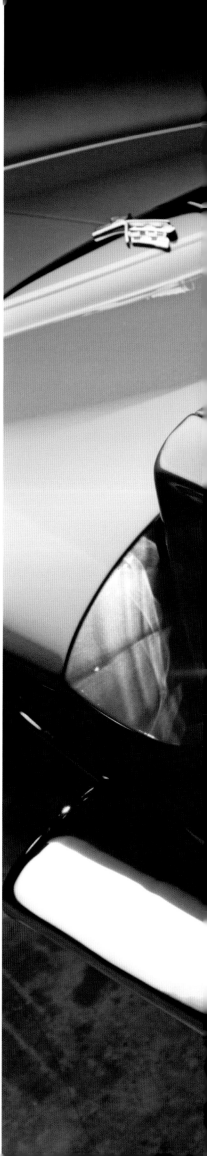

Frederick Donner's reaction to potential sales numbers for 1966 models proved to be a shrewd move, and it came none too soon. Ford Motor Company had respected the manufacturers' racing ban, and GM rigorously enforced it. Both companies surreptitiously supplied parts and support to racers, but Chrysler blatantly operated a revolving backdoor, delivering pieces and technology to racers. Henry Ford II had seen enough by early 1962, and he launched an aggressive project named "Total Performance: Powered by Ford." Ford jumped into all types of racing, and finally GM rejoined the fray. However, just because GM's board allowed no racing didn't mean progress and development stopped. When the gloves came off, Chevrolet (and Pontiac) division had ideas and engines to return to road circuits and quarter-mile strips, and had plans to titillate those customers who longed for greater excitement and neck-snapping acceleration.

Chevrolet offered five optional engines to supplement the 327–cubic inch, 300-horsepower base model. A 327 variation delivered 350 horsepower. The 427–cubic inch L36 held steady at 390 horsepower; a new L68 provided 400 horses; the L71 put out 435 horsepower; and a curious and very expensive L88 boasted 430.

It was a curiosity. The 435-horsepower L71 sold for $437.10—not a small sum in those days. But this L88, rated at 5 horsepower *less*, went for $947.90. That was no typographical error. In fact it was another example of shrewd marketing. The L88 was the engine for people who knew what it was, a pure racing creation that had very poor manners on regular streets. Racing regulations required Chevrolet to offer even its most potent products to every buyer in order to meet production quotas necessary for competition-class designations. So Chevy engineers and product planners slapped a high price on the L88 to deter those who did not know enough to avoid ordering something they did not really want. Rumors at the time (and even decades later) hinted at output greater than 480 horsepower, more than 530, even beyond 560, and attained at 6,000 rpm. Twenty cars left St. Louis with that powerplant in 1967.

C3

BEGINNING WITH ITS EUROPEAN STYLE sports car derivation—even its name, "Corvette," which refers to a nimble English warship—this car paid homage to the vehicle type and its origins. The third-generation Corvette moved through a period of muscle car virility when, on a universal scale, the United States *did* save the entire world from Communism. As the Corvette arrived in 1953, we were in a "police action" in Korea. As the car entered its second generation in 1963, we were gearing up for a "police action" in Southeast Asia. We had won the big war and now we were the world's cops, the strong man on the planet. Russia may have beaten us into space, launching a beach ball-sized satellite in 1957, but we could beat them in a quarter-mile any time, and that was the contest that meant much more to many car buyers.

As the Cold War lingered on, and after Mideast oil producers rattled their sabers and shut off their spigots, the Corvette evolved again. C3s softened

their shark-like aggressive edges into porpoise-like organic curves. Some social commentators have suggested the car became a symbol of Studio 54–era hedonism and laissez-faire economics. But its identity frequently had confused observers outside of GM and within: Was it a car for boulevard cruisers, or race-track tigers? That was a question even Chevy division manager Ed Cole couldn't answer in 1955, and this indecision led it to become a fashion accessory through the late 1970s and early 1980s when federal regulations made high performance a part of the car's history. The Corvette stalled for over a decade when GM's funding managers found other needs for their resources, but then just as America got interested in strength training when private gyms and health clubs sprung up, the C3 cleaned up its aerodynamics, added front and rear spoilers, and stretched out its back window, turning the late-life third generation Corvette into a mature and fit long-distance runner.

9

1968
L88
Convertible

1968
L88
Coupe

Corvette's anxiously awaited a "new design," which appeared for the 1968 model year. But its arrival was eventful and almost disastrous. Chevrolet had introduced its Camaro in 1967, a product essential to compete with Ford's ultra-successful Mustang. This car had needed extra attention as it reached the development finishing line, and those needs required GM to delay the Corvette to 1968.

IT SHOULDN'T HAVE BEEN that great a challenge. While Zora Duntov had advocated vigorously for a new chassis for the visually startling cars, cost considerations stopped any possibility. Corvette, with its poor early sales performance, had already become the corporation's flashy pariah. And Duntov, who arrived at Chevrolet in 1953 as an outspoken engineer, had become combative over the years. He fired off an angry memo to Chevrolet chief engineer Alex Mair. Duntov had achieved favorable results from many of his memos in the past; his words had fallen on open and receptive minds. But 15 years of it had rankled some in management who decided this latest rant crossed the line. In response, they closed the dedicated Corvette engineering department and reassigned the personnel. Many went to other passenger car or truck projects. Duntov found himself working in PR. Unfortunately for Chevrolet, this happened at the time final engineering checklists should have been cleared off. Early cars went out to media representatives as production geared up, and it became clear that GM had cut corners. The most provocative and damaging review came from *Car & Driver* magazine, which had scheduled to publish its review midwinter of 1967. "We won't," wrote Editor Steve Smith in his opening pages. "The car was unfit for a road test." He referred to "the car's shocking lack of quality control. With less than 2,000 miles on it, the Corvette was falling apart."

Chevrolet's division manager Pete Estes reopened the department and promoted Duntov to be Corvette's chief engineer. A year later, a *Car & Driver* readers' poll named the 1968 Corvette "best all-around car in the world."

Model year 1968 proved to be Corvette's most successful to date. St. Louis assembled 28,566 coupes and convertibles in all. Coupes allowed owners to remove roof panels and the rear window for a sense of open-air motoring. While overall sales from 1967 to 1968 increased by about 20 percent, sales of the L88 engine—still priced at $947.60—quadrupled, from 20 in 1967 to 80 throughout 1968. By this time, word had spread about what the engine was—temperamental, but very powerful—and demand increased among racers and those who competed on the street.

Over the three years that Chevrolet's Tonawanda engine assembly plant manufactured the L88, only 216 left the plant installed in Corvettes. This small number is a significant element in what has propelled the intense desirability and collectability of these uncommon cars. Engine compression was 12.5:1, which required using racing fuels with octane ratings above 105 RON. The forged crankshaft, solid valve lifters, and cold-air induction to ensure a denser fuel-air mix fed through an 850 cubic-feet-per-minute Holley four-barrel carburetor helped achieve the 550 horsepower at 6,200 rpm that most racers knew the engine developed without breaking a sweat. This made these cars extremely temperamental in routine driving conditions, and became a large part of the reason Chevrolet set such a high price for them. Chevrolet meant to discourage amateurs from buying something meant only for professionals.

On top of that, because Zora Duntov and his engineers conceived the powerplant for racing purposes, they eliminated a carburetor choke to assist with cold weather starting; removed the cooling fan shroud; and they deleted the heating and defrosting plumbing and mechanisms. No radio was available for the L88 models, though Chevrolet did offer a strengthened M20 Hydramatic transmission. Most L88 buyers opted for the heavy duty Muncie-built four-speed known as the M22 "Rock Crusher" for its durability and the noise it made in the cold.

Depending on final drive gearing, the L88s routinely ran quarter-mile acceleration times of 10.8 seconds and trap speeds of 156 miles per hour. Coupes and roadsters geared for endurance racing at tracks such as Daytona and Sebring regularly saw top speeds above 170 miles per hour.

The L88s represented singular time in American automobile marketing when a buyer who knew the necessary option codes was "allowed" to purchase a near-ready-to-race automobile from a major manufacturer. Naturally, racers typically gutted the already-minimal interior, reworked suspension systems and brakes, and installed rollover protection. Still, the L88 package got them at least 80 percent of the way to a competitive finish on the racetrack.

The L88 did not disappear at the end of 1969 model year because demand disappeared. If anything, the trajectory of its production growth from 20 units in 1967 to 80 in 1968 to 116 in 1969 suggest that Chevrolet might have produced 125 to 150 for 1970. However, because it was a regular production option, this engine had to meet exhaust emission standards for 1970, and this was impossible to do without strangling the power to levels that made it uncompetitive. When these engines dropped off Corvette order forms at the end of 1969, racers knew it was still possible to buy and build performance at or beyond this level. But for performance enthusiasts, unanswerable questions arose as to whether their favorite cars would again ever develop 400 horsepower or more.

10

1969
L71
Convertible

It is remarkable to think about Corvette's history of its first 15 years. By the time business closed on 1968 model year, Chevrolet had manufactured nearly 100 times as many Corvettes as it had in 1953.

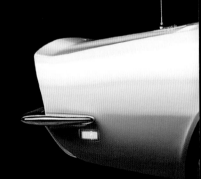

THE CAR HAD TEETERED on the edge of extinction a year later, and while production crept up to 3,640, more than 1,000 cars lingered into the new model year (1955), parked on the grounds of the car's new home in St. Louis. At the close of business for model year 1969, production reached 38,762, more than ten times what that dark, pivotal year had been. (A four-month labor strike at St. Louis let Chevrolet recalibrate its calendar, and new manager John DeLorean—to boost his production numbers—ran the Bowtie division model year longer than other GM divisions.) The car had been profitable for a decade, and 1969 numbers made every board member from the 1950s proud that it was the *other* guy on the board who had wanted to kill it.

Curiously, the 1968 model appeared wearing only a Corvette nameplate. The Sting Ray was gone. More curiously, a *Stingray* badge returned for 1969. Prices changed little between the two years—the base coupe went from $4,663 to $4,781, and convertibles inched up from $4,320 to $4,438. But the production figures reveal an interesting trend shift. The clever innovation that Corvette stylist Larry Shinoda and his studio manager Hank Haga devised with the coupe's removable roof and back window showed customers they could have open-top driving in the warm weather and an air-conditioned or heated-and-defrosted coupe in hot and cold conditions. Convertible production had always been the mainstay of Corvette output; it reached 16,633, still a respectable quantity. But the coupe hit 22,129. Tastes changed. And it was not until the Corvette's 50th anniversary in 2003 that convertible product reclaimed the lead—a distinction it held for that year only.

Corvette's engine lineup changed slightly. The base engine displacement grew from 327 cubic inches to create another legendary GM small-block designation: 350. All four 427s continued. The Tonowanda engine plant in New York manufactured 10,531 of the 390-horsepower L36, 2,072 of the 400-horsepower L68, 2,722 of the 435 horsepower L71, and 116 of the potent L88s. Aluminum cylinder heads, coded L89, hinted at other things on the option list, and 390 sets of them left Tonowanda on L71 engines. These made no horsepower difference, but the aluminum heads saved almost 40 pounds in weight on the front of the car.

A more significant weight advantage came at an extraordinary cost. Chevrolet engineer Frank Winchell and Corvette chief Zora Duntov nurtured through development an all-aluminum block 427, coded ZL-1, offered at $4,718.35 *plus* the price of the car. Most of these engines disappeared into Chevy Nova models intended for drag racing. While common lore reported that Chevrolet assembled only two ZL-1 engine Corvettes, engineer Ken Kayser (author of the definitive Rochester fuel-injection history book) was on staff at the Tonowanda plant from 1968 until his retirement in 1993, and, he knew there were seven. However, they were challenging engines to run at anything less than full throttle.

With this one beautiful exception, there is no such thing as a true American sports car.

'69 Corvette CHEVROLET

107

"One went to George Heberling. He was Corvette plant chief engineer in St. Louis," Kayser said. "This was the yellow coupe. Another went to Walt Witholz, who was the resident engineer at Tonowanda, the white one. But neither of the men liked the cars. Heberling routinely experienced *hydrolock* (the condition in which the engine seizes because uncompressable liquid blocks piston travel), and after several bouts with tow trucks and engine rebuilds, he turned the car in. It went into the executive pool, and a number of those guys checked the car out for a weekend, only to have it towed in, also hydrolocked. Then the cars just sat until they got sold.

"Zora had the cars assembled at St. Louis and the order came to St. Louis to quarantine the cars. Then the request came to me in Tonowanda to ship five L88 complete engines to St. Louis. St. Louis was supposed to pull the aluminum engines, install the L88s, and ship me the five remaining ZL-1 engines in exchange. But the ZL-1s never arrived.

"At year end, I was doing the accounting for replacement engines sent to St. Louis and the question came up: Where are the ZL-1 engines or where is payment?

"Turns out the plant manager always put quarantined cars in an enclosure at the back. He walked by and asked when these cars were going to be repaired and shipped out to dealers. It was coming up on year-end and he kept pressuring his guys. Get those cars out of here. Get those cars out." Then it appears another order came in.

"Everybody was dragging their feet," Kayser continued. "Then just before year-end, a couple of assembly line guys came in and sprayed the aluminum engines—in the cars—to look like L88s. And they went out the door on a truck to Zora.

"And from there? To friends. To racers. To who knows who? They knew what they had. But would somebody now who opens the hood and sees orange?"

When you play with numbers, strange results can emerge. When GM promoted Chevrolet Division Manager Pete Estes to corporate VP, it moved John DeLorean into Estes' former job. DeLorean had authorized installing a big Pontiac engine into a small Pontiac car—he called it the GTO. Acknowledging that cleverness, GM Chairman James Roche installed DeLorean in Chevy's top post.

THE PRODUCTION STRIKE during 1969 gave DeLorean an opportunity to manage his assembly totals, a key figure in assessing division success. This calculation resulted in St. Louis achieving its largest output ever. Understandably, this led to the adjustment year 1970, when totals shrunk to numbers not seen since solid axles drove Corvettes. Production at St. Louis ended at 10,668 coupes and 6,648 convertibles for a combined 17,316 units. Not knowing the background might lead a collector, an enthusiast, or a historian to misinterpret the numbers and attribute greater or lesser importance to this year. It really was nothing more than a boss playing with numbers.

Corvette body engineers paid attention to a complaint heard often about the 1968 and '69 cars. The F70-15 tires, mounted on 15x8J rims, were wide enough to routinely kick up rocks and debris, scratching and scoring the body sides. The front and rear tracks were 58.7 and 59.4 inches, respectively, compared to body width (69 inches at the beltline). To remedy that, styling and engineering flared out the fenders to capture more of the flying objects.

This was a subtle acknowledgement of Corvette owners' pride of ownership from a corporation that expected nothing less from Cadillac owners, anticipated it from Oldsmobile buyers, and hoped for it from Buick owners. This concept came together alongside the idea of the "personal luxury car." That new designation began to change Chevrolet's definition of the Corvette when it introduced an uncoded "Custom Interior Trim" option at $158.00. This package provided buyers leather on seating surfaces, a higher-quality carpet in the foot wells and luggage storage, and wood graining on the door panels and center console. It appealed to 3,191 buyers. A tide was turning, but few besides the product planners had noticed.

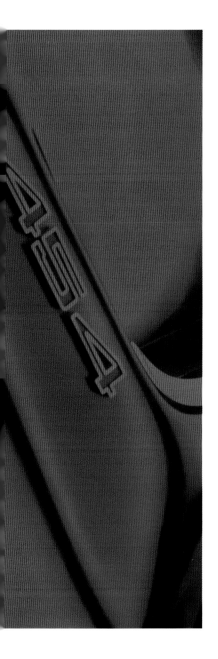

Performance unquestionably remained the Corvette's reason for being at this time. While emissions standards were starting to compromise engine output and vehicle acceleration, Chevrolet still offered engines ranging from the 350–cubic inch, 300-horsepower standard to the 350-horsepower 350, then to a Zora-inspired 370-horsepower, 350–cubic inch engine with solid valve lifters, and finally to the LS5, a monstrously torque-laden 454–cubic inch engine that developed—according to factory literature—390 horsepower. The truth was out there, and the 4,473 buyers who checked that option learned that this number was extremely conservative.

Visually, the 1970s models assumed a level of subtlety and sophistication that caught the attention of European journalists and then buyers, especially in France, a country that had long enjoyed powerful American cars. Bill Mitchell's stylists gave the car an egg-crate or ice cube tray–inspired front grille and a similar treatment to the side fender louvers. This reminded some buyers of the understated trim pieces on Ferraris and Maseratis of the period.

Prices slowly crept upwards, but this was inevitable. The base price from 1969 of $4,781 for the coupes and $4,438 for convertibles crossed the $5,000 barrier for coupes, reaching $5,192. Convertibles hunkered below that at $4,849 base price. But as engineers and stylists dealt with emissions and safety standards, the planners already had noticed they might need to reconsider the car's purpose.

12

1971
LT1
Coupe

1971
LS6
Convertible

The LT1 ZR1 was another of the engine/chassis performance packages that became a legend in Corvette history. It evolved into the inspiration of later Corvette marketing and model designations.

CHEVROLET INTRODUCED the 350–cubic inch LT1 engine for the 1970 model year. This emerged from Duntov's dissatisfaction with the philosophy that Corvette product planners had to put ever and ever larger displacement—and heavier—engines into *his* car.

The "ZR1" legend has—as all great legends should—an origin story. GM Chairman Frederick Donner had retired. He had authored and then rescinded the racing ban. He had banned and then embraced huge displacement, high-powered engines in GM's midsize (and even compact) cars. This whole era was a pursuit of numbers. For drag racers, it was elapsed time from start to the end of the quarter-mile. For oval or road-course competitors, it was lap times. For Donner, it was sales figures and profits.

GM's board of directors recognized that Duntov's former boss, Ed Cole, had produced very good numbers for two decades. They promoted him to president of the company. He served under another Donner-type, another profits-oriented leader named James Roche. Roche rose through the corporate ranks watching Donner and Cole. One provided what the other needed. And, towards the end, vice versa.

Car and Driver Readers' Choice Poll:
1971: Best all-around car.
1970: Best all-around car.
1969: Best all-around car.
1968: Best all-around car.
If we said any more, we'd be bragging.

Corvette
by Chevrolet

Corvette performance starts with AC

Performance under the hood of a Corvette starts with AC.

It's been going on since the Corvette was first-introduced! For good reason.

Corvette has an outstanding reputation for performance to maintain. That's one of the reasons why AC ACniter Spark Plugs are installed as original equipment. ACs heat fast, fire hot to help burn away fouling deposits.

Corvettes come off the assembly line with AC Air and Oil Filters for top engine protection.

And with AC Fuel Pumps that help eliminate fuel starvation even under demanding acceleration.

Corvette goes with the best. You should, too. See your nearby AC dealer for these and other outstanding AC automotive parts. You'll be in great company.

120

Cole's ideas sold Chevrolets. The largest corporate division buoyed the entire ship. And if Cole said a small-block engine with a sophisticated valvetrain and high performance for the Corvette was going to sell additional units, Roche accepted Cole's word.

The legend that is ZR1 also has myths. And those suggest that this regular production option (RPO) code stands for "Zora Racer type One." Chevrolet introduced it in 1970, and when a big-block version appeared in 1971, when most Duntov-watchers knew he had made peace with the heavy front engines (after all, he had one in his own car that year), the ZR2 with its 454–cubic inch engine was surely "Zora Racer type Two."

The 1970 ZR1 provided buyers with a 350–cubic inch engine equipped with solid valve lifters and developing 370 horsepower. It was an expensive option, priced at $968.95, but it provided those who understood option specifications with the Muncie M22 "Rock Crusher" four-speed gearbox, heavy-duty power brakes, transistorized ignition for better combustion, an aluminum radiator to reduce weight up front, and front and rear springs and shocks adapted and improved from the earlier road racing option packages. Only 25 buyers believed they needed these options in 1970.

For 1971, the price jumped to $1,010, the production numbers plummeted to eight, and engine output—now affected by GM's early efforts to anticipate the effects of introducing unleaded gasoline with its lower octane ratings—dropped to 330 horsepower. Those who wanted the still-potent, solid-lifter LT1 without the other "racey" ZR1 pieces numbered a respectable 1,949 buyers who paid $483 for the sweet-sounding engine.

At the other end of the spectrum, Chevrolet's LS6 454–cubic inch, 425-horsepower cost buyers three times as much ($1,221) yet it still attracted 188 buyers. As Mike Antonick reported in his *Corvette Black Book*, "The 454ci LS6 engine was a detuned version of 1970's planned but cancelled 460hp LS7. LS6 was designed to operate on low-lead fuel, but since a comparable engine was not available in 1970, it won the horsepower race for the two years despite its lower octane rating. It featured aluminum heads and could be ordered with an automatic transmission, although not when combined with the ZR2 package." Only 12 customers opted for the ZR2 package that included all ZR1 equipment with the larger displacement engine.

Total production in 1971 model year, readjusted following DeLorean's manipulations, reached 21,801 Corvettes. Of these, 14,680 were coupes, and convertible production amounted to 7,121 cars. But few people who bought Corvette's largest-displacement, highest-output engines in model year 1971 had squinted into the future. Fewer still saw what was coming in 1972.

Even through model year 1973, American car owners and performance enthusiasts thought their worst enemy was the U.S. Department of Transportation (US DOT) and the US Environmental Protection Agency (US EPA) No one yet had heard of that other "letters" group—OPEC, or the Organization of Petroleum-Exporting Countries. In October 1973, as buyers took delivery of their 1974 models, OPEC raised its ugly head.

13 1975 CONVERTIBLE

The American Heritage Dictionary defines *paranoia* as "extreme, irrational distrust of others." It has led individuals and corporations to do extreme, irrational acts.

THERE IS NO DOUBT that consumer advocate Ralph Nader knocked the American automobile industry off its feet with his searing indictment of GM's failure to produce a better Corvair. The corporation then made further mistakes in handling Nader, and this inspired a voter-conscious US Congress to propose actions it estimated would save lives and votes.

Rules and reality for American carmakers changed in October 1973 when the Organization of Petroleum Exporting Countries (OPEC) dramatically upset the traditional equations of demand for oil and its supply. That same year, US federal crash standards mandated that vehicle front bumpers survived a five–mile per hour front impact without damage. This forced designers and engineers from every automaker to re-engineer the fronts of their cars. After considerable experimentation and testing, Chevrolet engineers devised a honeycomb framework attached to the car over which they stretched a composite urethane material.

This period marked the start of the next transformation in the Corvette's nature. It began the evolution from sports car/muscle car to "personal" car, from a two-seater with proven and demonstrable performance credentials to an intimate and exclusive luxury automobile. GM's product planners and especially those working on Corvettes recognized what the coming fuel economy, exhaust emission, and vehicle and passenger safety requirements meant for a lightning-fast sports car. Through 1974, the Corvette continued this shift, morphing into a real grand-touring automobile in an American sense. The speed limit dropped to 55 miles per hour across the United States, but that didn't mean drivers had to sacrifice the sense of accomplishment and of exclusivity that Corvette ownership implied.

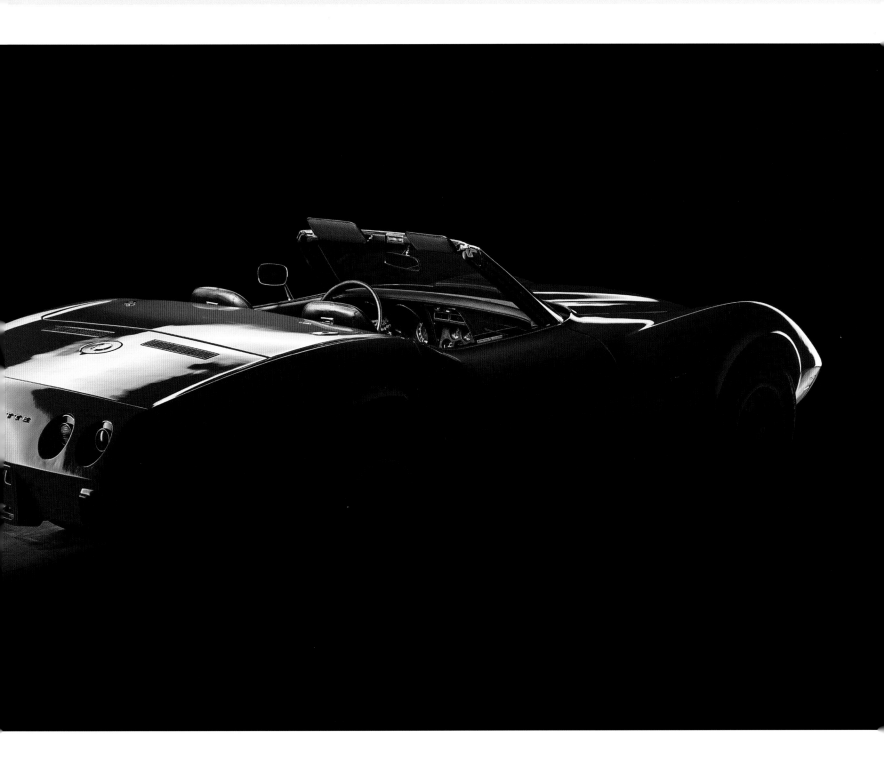

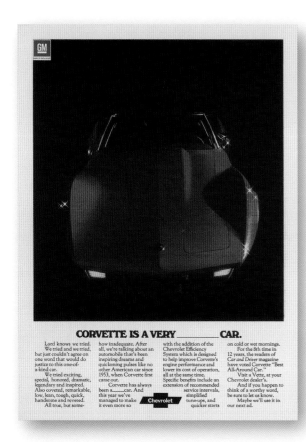

Model year 1975 was loaded with significant passings. Zora Duntov retired at 65, GM's mandatory age. GM also retired its convertibles, including the Corvette. As Ralph Nader's raiders looked for new horizons to challenge, the "rollover safety standards" of America's soft-top cars made everyone nervous. Before Congress acted, the nervous automakers moved pre-emptively. Where Corvette's early days had suggested that all sports cars were convertibles, open-car sales of Corvettes in 1974 had been about one-in-seven. For 1975, it barely reached one-in-eight. And then there were none.

Engine output also suffered in these times. Rising gas prices made huge displacement and enormous horsepower a liability at least financially speaking. The base Corvette left St. Louis with a 165-horsepower, 350–cubic inch engine and a wide-ratio, four-speed manual transmission. Buyers chose the Turbo-Hydramatic or the close-ratio, four-speed manual as no-extra-cost options. And the only engine upgrade provided 205 horsepower from the 350 engine for $336. But because that didn't include the cost for extra gas consumed, just 2,372 of the car's 38,465 total production drove out of St. Louis with the "big" engine. Those days were gone. Enthusiasts began to fear they were gone forever.

By the time 1978 arrived, the near-death days of Corvette's early existence in 1953 and 1954 felt much further away than they had two decades ago. Chevrolet division felt a major birthday celebration was well earned as St. Louis assembly had manufactured an astonishing 49,213 coupes through 1977, calculations made over a 12-month calendar, not DeLorean's exaggerated 16-month stretch. What's more, after slightly more than a decade of the third-generation Corvette introduced in 1968, it was time for a facelift.

YET DESPITE ITS EVER-INCREASING SALES, there was little money available for restyling. The most affordable, easiest, and quickest change was to redesign the roof. Stylists trimmed the deep "flying buttresses" that trailed off from the C-3's B-pillar, and they installed a large contoured back window. Some of Bill Mitchell's first concepts for the C-3 had looked like this with the addition of a functioning hatchback/opening rear glass panel. In celebrating 25 years of life, designers and engineers wanted to introduce that feature for 1978. But engineering considerations—especially those caused by the 15-year-old transverse leaf-spring indepen-

The rear window plan went through, and this brought more light into the cockpit and banished the cave-like feeling few earlier owners had cherished. With a subtle front chin spoiler and the angled "ducktail" on the rear, chief engineer Dave McLellan and his staff reduced the Corvette's coefficient of drag, Cd, from 0.50 to 0.42.

As the 1978 model facelift moved through design and engineering, Bill Mitchell prepared for retirement. He told Corvette chief designer Jerry Palmer that he wanted to commemorate the 25 years of Corvette with a special treatment, using his favorite car color, silver, as the basis for a Silver Anniversary model. Palmer added his signature to the package with a red stripe around the "beltline" to separate it from the charcoal gray lower body.

Around this time, Chevrolet public relations staff approached officials at the Indianapolis Motor Speedway to propose they use this Silver Anniversary car to pace the race. Board Chairman Tony Hulman and his directors agreed, and Chevrolet began to publicize the arrival of a special edition of the 1978 Corvette. But unbeknownst to enthusiasts, Chevrolet asked Hulman and his board to select the color scheme, and they created the black-over-silver design. It proved to be a shrewd decision for it let Chevrolet market three versions of the coupe as a base model, a silver anniversary commemorative, and an Indianapolis 500 Pace Car replica. These variations led to another high output year, and St. Louis assembled 46,766 Corvettes for 1978 model year, 6,502 of which were pace car replicas and 15,283 were anniversary cars. Base price for the coupe was $9,351.89. The silver anniversary paint scheme—delivered with alloy wheels, as was the pace car—added $399 to the total, while the pace car sold for $13,653.21, the first time a Corvette price topped $10,000.

The standard 350–cubic inch V-8 offered 185 horsepower, but an optional L82 delivered 220 horsepower for an additional $525. Buyers had a choice at no additional charge of either a close-ratio, four-speed manual gearbox or an automatic transmission with deliveries of automatics outnumbering manuals by nearly 12 to 1.

SECTION THREE:

C4 AND C5

IN 1984, THE NEW C4 CORVETTE emerged as the American interpretation of the high-performance automobile. We had made the concept our own. The Corvette was different from, less costly than, and fully equal to all but the rarest sports cars the world had to offer. When the ZR1 appeared, Chevrolet took the car to France in late 1989 for the worldwide media introduction, showing European carmakers on their own turf what America had done. With the arrival of the "King of the Hill," as magazine journalists dubbed the powerful but understated model, the Corvette endorsed its Jekyll-and-Hyde nature as both boulevard cruiser and racetrack—or Autobahn—tiger.

Through the car's three generations to this point, it had been a product of the dynamic personalities that became its champions even as they contested one another for supremacy of influence. Generation one models pitted the car's creator, Harley Earl, against its adopted uncle, Zora Duntov. While both wanted the car to succeed, their views of its identity aided and abetted Ed Cole's dilemma: boulevardier or racer? Earl retired, and his handpicked successor Bill Mitchell proved even more difficult for GM's board to manage and for Zora Duntov to manipulate. But it was Mitchell's designers and stylists who created Corvette's most striking lines. This work and his influence on sales across all of the corporation's product lines solidified Mitchell's power.

Generation three brought in Dave McLellan to replace Duntov when Zora retired, and the brilliant and pragmatic engineer who served under Duntov had learned it's easier to push a rock along a level playing field than uphill. Under his direction, the car not only became a much faster boulevardier keeping up with Europe's finest, but it also challenged them head-to-head on America's race courses.

With the arrival of C4, another voice emerged, that of designer John Cafaro, whose clean, almost architectural shapes and forms represented a substantial change in design language from the undersea organics of Mitchell and his staff. Cafaro's body had many more systems to cloak, and the car grew even as its proportions remained clearly Corvette. Cafaro made those forms more taut, more graceful, and more eye-catching with his C5—the new generation presented a dramatic change in visual impact. At the same time, engineering chief Dave Hill updated the car with engines and electronic suspension systems that kept it on par with any other competitor. Their 50th Anniversary model represented for many enthusiasts their "lifetime achievement" award. Chevrolet sold thousands of the 2003 models to middle-aged first-time Corvette buyers. The dreams of Earl and Duntov, Mitchell and McLellan culminated in the anniversary commemorative and the raucous, muscular, in-your-face Z06.

15

1989
L71
Convertible

Chevrolet reintroduced the convertible Corvette for model year 1986 after discontinuing the open cars at the end of 1975. Concerns about vehicle rollover safety and changing customer preferences led to the decision to discontinue the cars and changing customer preferences brought them back.

ALONG WITH THE manual collapsing cloth top, Chevrolet introduced a removable hardtop, regular production CC2, for $1,995. Of the 9,749 convertibles Chevrolet produced at its Bowling Green assembly plant, 1,573 went out with the optional hardtop. This one, in Bright Red with the Red base leather interior, went to a very discriminating Corvette customer, Zora Duntov.

Duntov, who retired in 1975, enjoyed management-retiree discounts on GM products and this convertible, purchased shortly before his 79th birthday, was his last Corvette. Duntov, who was born on Christmas Day 1909, died April 21, 1996.

Horsepower output, always a strong concern of Duntov's and one his successor, Dave McLellan, had slowly been creeping back up to reasonable levels after the performance dark ages of the late 1970s and early 1980s. This was the end of the C3 era, and cars of this period emphasized creature comforts and exclusivity since the startling performance of the late 1960s no longer was available. The C4, introduced in 1984, brought to Corvette buyers the next generation 350–cubic inch "Cross-Fire injection" V-8, designed and manufactured to meet all 1984 emissions and fuel-economy standards. Since the 1984 version appeared with 205 horsepower, Bosch electronic-tuned port injection and other engine improvements increased output to 230 horsepower for 1985. Aluminum cylinder heads appeared on late-introduction 1986 convertible and coupes, adding another 5 horsepower to the total while internal friction reductions for 1987 inched the output up yet another 5 horsepower to make 240. Less restrictive mufflers for coupes (only) in 1988 increased output 5 more horsepower to 245. Product planners considered the mufflers too loud for convertibles, but noise never bothered Duntov, who got the system on this car, making it one of the very few so equipped.

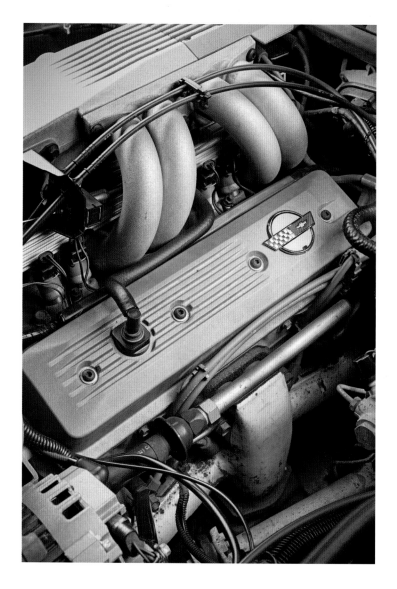

153

By this time, Duntov had shifted enough gears by himself, and he ordered the car with the standard four-speed automatic gearbox. Coincidentally most Corvette buyers agreed with Zora, and of the total of 26,412 coupes and convertibles manufactured for model year 1989, just 4,113 left Bowling Green with the new ZF computer-aided six-speed manual transmission. (This gearbox sensed throttle load, and under gentle acceleration its computers diverted the gear shift from first directly to fourth on upshifts. The engine's substantial torque easily accommodated this range. The transmission also blocked access to fifth and sixth gears under these conditions as well, in an effort to maintain fuel economy.)

Over his last years, Zora drove 35,500 miles in this car. He used it to get from his home in suburban Detroit to several events at the Bowling Green assembly plant and for the groundbreaking ceremony for the National Corvette Museum in June 1992.

154

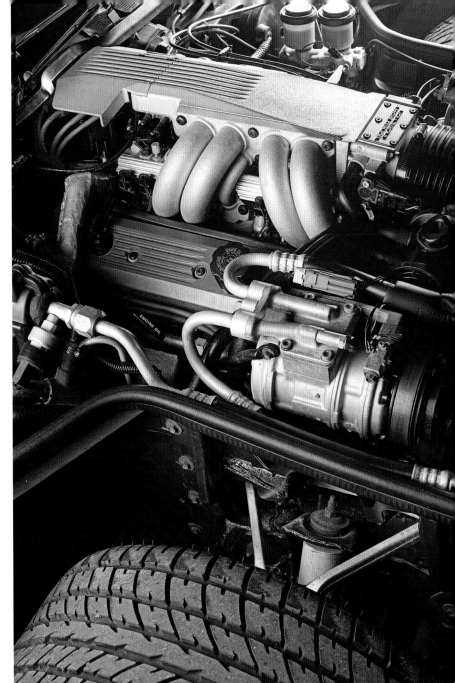

16

1995
ZR1
Coupe

This marked the end of the era, and this Competition Yellow coupe came extremely close to ending the ZR1 production run that began in 1990.

BOWLING GREEN and Stillwater, Oklahoma, home of the ZR1 engines, turned out 6,939 of these models over the six model-year span. In the last three years of production, 1993, 1994, and 1995, Mercury Marine, limited by its own manufacturing capacity, assembled 448 engines, completing the final round of them in November 1993 after which Bowling Green stored them in advance of installation. With assembly ending at 448 units in 1995, this yellow car was number 443. It was one of only 49 ZR1s delivered in Competition Yellow.

The original owner ordered the car very specifically, charting the rarity of the color scheme as the totals rose. When Bowling Green assembly shipped the car to his dealer, he insisted they neither clean it nor prepare it for delivery. As such, all its plastic shipping wrappers remained in place with their barcoded stickers unmolested. Between delivery in early calendar year 1995 and early April 2014 when these photos were made, the car had accumulated just 18 miles. The day after this shoot, the car went to its next owner, a car

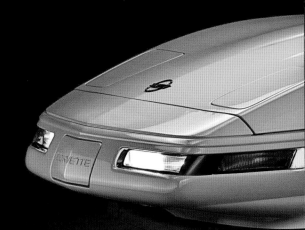

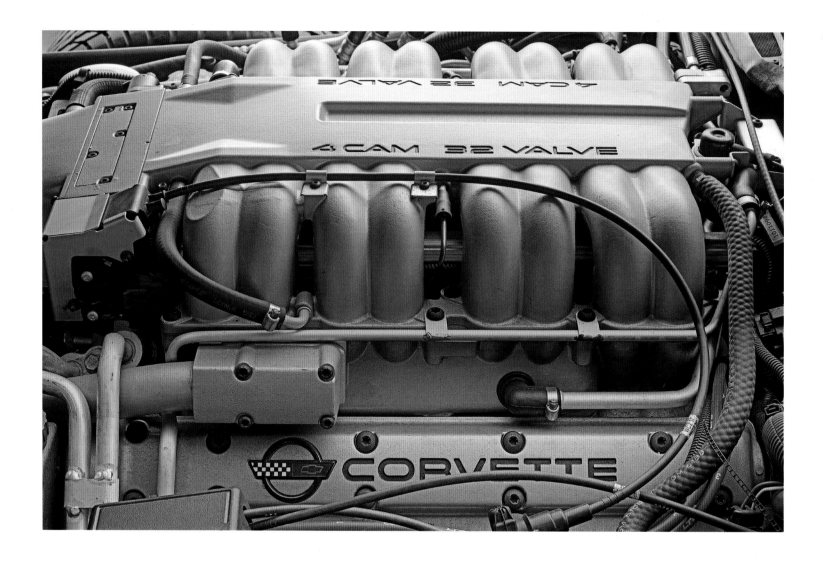

On one hand, it's a shame not to drive and enjoy the Corvette ZR1. Chevrolet debuted the cars to a huge media gathering in France in 1989 but chose not to release any production models for that year. For the first three production years, 1990, 1991, and 1992, the ZR1s built a generation of enthusiasts and loyalists for the soon-to-be-legendary LT5 V-8. With dual overhead camshafts (DOHC) and four valves per cylinder, the engine—jointly designed by Chevrolet and then-GM subsidiary Lotus Engineering in the UK—developed 375 horsepower. Following extensive internal modifications to cylinder heads and the DOHC valve gear, and a change to four-bolt main crankshaft bearings allowing higher engine speeds, output rose to 405 horsepower for its final three model years. With its startling performance and its top speed of more than 185 miles per hour, the car earned the nickname "King of the Hill."

In 1990, the inaugural ZR1 models looked remarkably undistinguished except for subtly flared rear fenders to accommodate much wider P315/35ZR17 rear tires on the 11-inch wide wheels. Buyers paid a premium of $27,016 on top of the base coupe price of $31,979, and some complained that for their $58,995, they wanted something more eye catching. Instead, Chevrolet gave all 1991 Corvette models the wider rear end, igniting some grumbling from ZR1 owners. Throughout its life, the C4 platform ZR1 kept all its distinctions underneath the skin.

In its final year the 405-horsepower model required a $31,285 optional commitment on top of the $36,785 base coupe price. That $68,070 guaranteed Chevrolet customers their spot in a niche of Corvette history. When ZR1 sales ended, no one had a clue that the model might return.

163

17

1996
GRAND SPORT
Coupe

This was an odd moment in Corvette history. Enthusiasts and the automotive media knew very well that a new Corvette, the long-delayed fifth-generation version, was coming as a 1997 model year introduction.

ON THE OTHER SIDE OF THE CALENDAR, 1995 had been the final year Corvette had offered its King of the Hill ZR1. Its supply of engines had run out, and its outside engine assembler had shipped the dies and entire manufacturing line back to Michigan. Corvette sales had survived the recession in 1991 and 1992 when production totals dipped to twenty-thousand-and-a-few cars, but it had begun rebounding slowly. Keeping momentum going—and keeping Bowling Green assemblers employed—was part of Chevrolet division strategy. But how?

The Bowtie division had learned that special editions motivated buyers. Starting with Indianapolis 500 Pace Car replicas and silver anniversary commemoratives in 1978, Chevrolet honored the car's 35th birthday in 1988, launched the ZR1 series in 1990, and followed that with special Callaway twin-turbo models beginning in 1991. Variety proved to be the spice of life for Corvette sales, and the carmaker and its customers were pouring it on in equal measure.

For 1996, Corvette planners resurrected a name from its 1963 racing effort with its ultra-lightweight, supremely powerful Grand Sport. They made it an option package, Z16, limited to 1,000 examples, and added $2,880 to the $45,060 price of a base convertible or $3,250 to the $37,225 base coupe. Production counted 810 coupes and 190 convertibles. Chevrolet delivered them in Admiral Blue paint—only—with a wide white "racing stripe" up and over the centerline of the car and a pair of red slashes on the driver's-side front quarter panel.

Engineers reworked the thoroughly proven 350–cubic inch LT1, revising the aluminum cylinder heads, redesigning the camshaft profiles, and installing Crane roller rocker arms to improve valve actuation. With other changes and improvements, including changes in the throttle body induction system, they managed to increase output from 300 horsepower in the LT1 to 330 horsepower in the newly designated LT4. This new engine was standard in the Grand Sport package, and buyers got six-speed manual transmissions with no automatic available. This combination got the car from 0 to 60 miles per hour in 5.0 seconds, through the quarter-mile in 13.5 seconds at 104 miles per hour, and on to a top speed of 168 miles per hour.

Chevrolet carried over the wide ZR1 wheels and tires onto this new model, using the 275/40ZR17 fronts and 315/35ZR17 rears on the ZR1's five spoke wheels on Grand Sport coupes, which sported added-on rear fender flares (unlike the ZR1 widened body rear quarter panels). Convertibles used 255/45 ZR17 fronts and 285/40ZR17 rears on bodies without the flared fenders. This accounted for some of the price difference. Chevrolet painted the wheels black for all the Grand Sport models.

Total production for the final year of the C4 platform topped out at 21,536 cars. Of these, 17,167 were coupes and 4,369 were convertibles, including the 1,000 Grand Sport versions.

18

2003
50TH ANNIV
Convertible

Model year 1997 brought the long-awaited fifth generation Corvette, C5. Where previous generations had carried over chassis or engines, this new car was all new. It even introduced the transaxle rear end, an innovation Zora Duntov had advocated and hoped for with the 1963 Sting Ray models.

A new 346–cubic inch (5.7-liter) LS1 engine drove the C5. It had a cast aluminum alloy block, cast aluminum oil pan, and cylinder heads. Its 345-horsepower peak output arrived at 5,600 rpm, and the engine developed 350 lb-ft of torque at 4,400 rpm.

Chevrolet marketing began planning for the Corvette's 50th anniversary almost as soon as the C5 appeared. Model year 2003 celebrated a half-century of the two-seater. To commemorate this accomplishment, the Bowtie division created the 1SC equipment group known as the 50th Anniversary package. This included Anniversary Red Xirallic Crystal exterior paint and a new Shale interior. It added in the bits and pieces from the 1SB preferred equipment group and a stunning new F55 Magnetic Selective Ride Control system with near instant response to ride and driving dynamics.

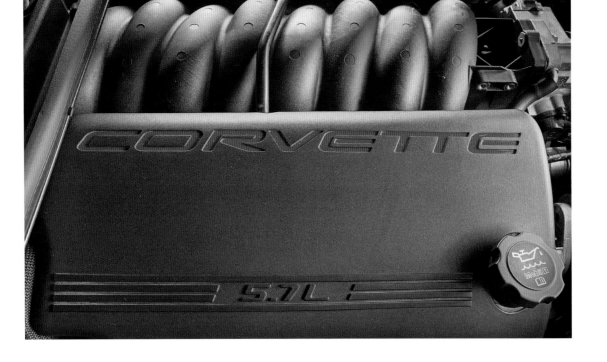
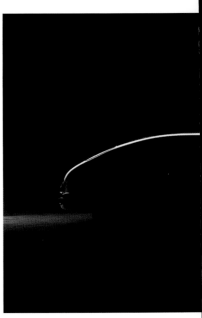

This system introduced innovative dampers—shock absorbers—filled with Magneto-Rheological fluid. Inside the piston of each damper, engineers had inserted an electromagnetic coil that, by varying current through the coil, served to increase or decrease the density of the fluid, resulting in, as Chevrolet's public relations information said at the time, "continuously variable real-time damping. As a result, drivers feel a greater sense of security; a quieter, flatter ride; and more precise, responsive handling, particularly during sudden high-speed maneuvers. Sensors read road conditions from all four tires, calculating road speed, lateral and longitudinal acceleration, steering wheel angle, suspension travel, and brake pedal angle to energize these dampers." It did this 1,000 times per second so effectively the system monitored changes in the road inch by inch. The F55 system offered two settings—Sport and Tour—delivering aggressive handling for those wanting race-car performance yet coddling the tired racer on the way home from the track with a comfortable, compliant ride. The system was standard on the 50th Anniversary commemoratives and optional on coupes and convertibles for $1,695.

The Corvette pace car for the Indianapolis 500 was a lightly modified 50th Anniversary coupe. Graphics packages—the only "replica" option available—were an additional $495.

Production figures—strong since C5 introduction—varied little with the commemorative edition. Bowling Green turned out 12,812 coupes of which 4,085 were the 50th Anniversary model. Another 14,022 convertibles emerged, and 7,547 of these were the commemoratives.

The 50th Anniversary Edition 1SC regular production option added $5,000 to the price of either the $43,895 base coupe or $50,370 base convertible.

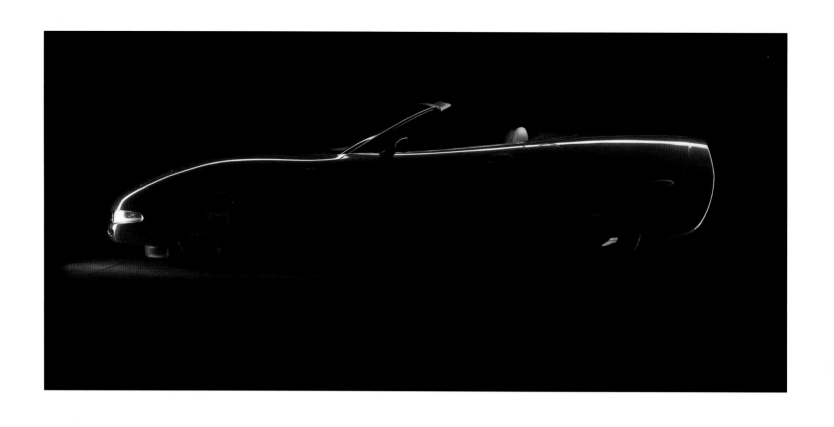

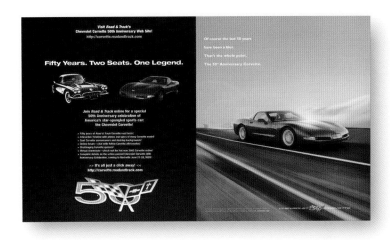

19

Back in the 1990s, as engineers, stylists, and management considered what the C5 was going to be, Chevrolet division General Manager Jim Perkins promoted the idea of an entry level model, a notchback, fixed-in-place hardtop that was distinctive yet affordably enticing to the first-time Corvette buyer. As time passed and his body-style concept moved through the process, his message of entry-level took a turn toward something much more potent.

The 2001 Z06 became a technological showplace, fitted with a titanium exhaust system and a larger hollow front stabilizer bar. Consistent efforts at materials management pulled dozens of pounds out of the car, but these upgrades and improvements altered the price structure radically. By 2001, the hardtop—available only as the Z06 model—had shot up to be Corvette's most expensive model at $47,500, putting it $500 above the convertible and $7,025 higher than the base coupe. This figure did not really dampen sales; Corvette customers were ready for a return to better performance. Out of total production of 35,627 cars, 5,773 were the Z06 hardtop.

Next year's Z06 became more formidable, with output reaching the earlier ZR1 level of 405 horsepower and torque climbing from 385 to 400 lb-ft. Innumerable changes and materials upgrades shaved weight from the Z06, and parts and pieces began to trickle into coupe and convertible models as well. Manufacturing numbers for 2002 suggested Chevrolet had taken the right direction with the Z06, which counted 8,297 units out of the combined 35,767 assembly total. The price drifted up to $50,150, crossing another threshold that quickly fell by the wayside.

Corvette continued the Z06 hardtop in the 50th anniversary year, although the special exterior paint and interior upholstery package was not available. The car retained its 405 horsepower, and modifications were negligible. Bowling Green output of the hardtop model held steady for a third year, at 8,635 cars out of 35,469 manufactured. The price held steady as well, increasing just $5 from the 2002 price of $51,150 to $51,155 for 2003.

SECTION FOUR:

C6 AND C7

SOME WRITERS HAVE CHARACTERIZED the sixth generation Corvettes (2005–2013) as among the least changed in the car's history, going so far as to designate it a C5.6 or 5.7, rather than C6. Its styling, its lines, forms, and shapes were steps—not leaps—from the trend-setting C5. That was what buyers and journalists saw. But no matter how jaded these observers might be, only blindness can keep them from acknowledging the countless under-skin engineering and engine revolutions that appeared throughout the C6 model run, culminating in the most powerful automobile GM has ever produced in any division—the 638 horsepower ZR1, introduced in 2009. This car—also GM's most expensive model—carried on with admirable consistency a long-standing Corvette styling characteristic: that of exhibiting only markedly subtle visual differentiation between its base model and its most exclusive, powerful, headline-grabbing variations. It's evidence of Corvette's own comfort and security within its "skin" that the car lets its performance announce its presence without appended fender flares or high-flying rear wings as marketing cues. Badges and understated hood treatments—Chevrolet's statements of choice since 1965—are all that inform other car owners that they are driving alongside a lesser or greater Corvette. These cars are the work of chief engineer Tadge Juechter and styling director Jerry Palmer, who each learned the ropes working with predecessors Dave Hill and John Cafaro. That the C6 is the extension of the C5 represents a carefully considered evolution.

With the C7, however, Juechter and Palmer hit their stride. As an engineering accomplishment, Juechter and his staff moved the benchmark far down the table with nearly every component on the car either extensively redesigned or replaced with new. Consider that Corvette's first buyer in Europe was neither some well-connected French enthusiast nor a well-connected transplant American aching to stretch the car out on a German autobahn. Instead, it was a certain German sports car company that regularly competes against Corvette in a number of international racing series. Their engineers admit they admire the car for its performance, for its weight management, and for its exceptional value for its price.

Visually, the car takes a very long evolutionary step from C6 and from the four generations that introduced and manipulated the coke-bottle taper. This is at its most dramatic and ornamented form in the new car. In many ways and in many views, the appearance is revolutionary because of the well-intended and cleverly executed respect for the family lineage. The light-painting technique used in this book sometimes clings to bodywork like well-blended paint, and other times it slips off like rainwater. Convex forms react differently to soft boxes and reflector lamps than do concave surfaces. Carefully sculpted body forms—both those on the sides and on the top surfaces of the C7 Stingray—catch, reflect, and play with the light, making it one of the most intriguing in the book to shoot. Just as with the finest of the Bill Mitchell–era Corvettes, the new 2014 Corvette Stingray offers visual entertainment to accompany its performance and handling.

20

2007
Z06
Coupe

Chevrolet introduced the sixth-generation Corvette series, the C6, with the 2005 model year. Given a new exterior and interior, the car operated on an updated and substantially revised C5 chassis. Corvette engineers lengthened the wheelbase 1.2 inches from 104.5 to 105.7, and trimmed overall length by a considerable 5.1 inches (while narrowing it 1.1 inches). These changes improved ride comfort yet did not compromise interior space or handling.

UNDER THE HOOD, the new LS2 displaced 364 cubic inches and developed 400 horsepower and 400 lb-ft of torque. The six-speed manual or four-speed automatic were no-cost choices, and two-thirds of the introductory year C6 buyers—22,380 out of 37,372 total production—opted to let the machine and its brains do their thinking and shifting.

The Z06 model returned for 2006, and it offered buyers vast amounts of high technology for its substantial price. Using a unique aluminum frame, magnesium engine cradle, and, as Mike Antonick in his *Corvette Black Book*, referred to it, "a magnesium-supported fixed roof panel," the "Z06's frame, as supplied by Dana Corp, was 30 percent lighter than its steel counterpart."

The LS7 aluminum block displaced 427 cubic inches and developed 505 horsepower. Such changes under the hood and under the skin made the Z06 essentially a different car from the base Corvette coupe. This, in combination with the lighter chassis and body, weighing 3,132 pounds on the road, offered buyers 0-to-60–mile per hour acceleration in 3.7 seconds. The base coupe sold for $44,600, and the altogether more potent Z06 sold for $65,800. Bowling Green assembled 6,272 of the Z06 models, 11,151 convertibles, and 16,598 coupes for a total of 34,021 cars.

Despite a pair of price increases to the Z06 for 2007 model year (up to $66,465, and then on to $70,000), sales of the high performer increased to 8,159 units. Of this, 399 were a special commemorative edition honoring accomplished Corvette racer Ron Fellows. With the American economy surging along, it took Corvette sales and manufacturing totals with it. Bowling Green finished the year counting 21,484 coupes and 10,918 convertibles in addition to the combined Z06 production. The aggregate was 40,561 Corvettes, giving Chevrolet its second best Corvette year up to that time (but about 11,000 units behind the 1984 C4 introduction year at 51,547).

With the exception of 2004, final year of the C5 generation, most Z06 customers chose black for their exterior color, sometimes by as much as two-to-one over other choices, buyers perhaps preferring to emphasize the stealthy and sinister look of the model. The 2004 model—a special Le Mans commemorative—sold most in what Chevrolet called "Lemans [sic] Blue." In that year it almost doubled the black cars sales figures at 2,025 compared to 1,186 cars.

CHEVY CORVETTE Available as a coupe, convertible, or the legendary Z06. Living up to its performance-enhanced shredding 505 horsepower. It propels the Z06 to 60 mph in 3.7 seconds and down the quarter mile in 11.7 seconds at 125 mph. roots, the Z06 comes standard with a hand-built 7.0L aluminum-block engine. We call it the LS7, and it churns out a pavement-Plus, with undeniable grip, it carves 1.04g on the skidpad. chevy.com **AN AMERICAN R VOLUTION**

AND THEN HE GAVE ME THREE WISHES...

21

2012 ZR1 Coupe

Chevrolet resurrected the ZR1 option code on the Corvette for the 2009 model year, creating, in a single automobile, three significant GM product distinctions.

FIRST, THE ZR1 took the fundamental 6.2-liter, 376–cubic inch LS3 engine, performed a number of internal modifications, and fitted it with a Roots-type supercharger and an intercooler. This changed the designation to LS9 and boosted output from base 430 horsepower to 638. It earned the engine the distinction as GM's highest output engine ever. Second, this power and a few other improvements cut 0-to-60–mile per hour acceleration to 3.1 seconds and elevated the ZR1's top speed to 205 miles per hour, the highest terminal velocity ever for a GM product. Third, all this performance and all these improvements did not come cheap, and Chevrolet division priced the car at $103,300, the first time a Corvette (not a Callaway conversion) crested the $100K summit.

This power was manageable only with Chevrolet's enhanced and strengthened six-speed transmission. The ZR1 started life on the aluminum chassis of the Z06 model, but engineers fitted it with the updated magnetic ride control it had introduced on the 2003 50th Anniversary commemoratives. Engineers also determined that the ZR1 needed enormous Brembo disc brakes—with 15.5-inch diameter front rotors and 15.0-inch rears—to haul the car down from such high speeds. They fitted six-piston front calipers and four-piston units on the rear wheels.

Proud of the technologically advanced engine and intercooler, stylists incorporated a clear polycarbonate "window" in the carbon fiber front deck lid to reveal the intercooler. They painted the rest of the hood and the carbon fiber front fenders in body color while they left the fixed-roof panel in unpainted carbon. In 2009, Bowling Green assembly produced 1,415 of the cars, though they suffered a $1,700 gas guzzler tax penalty. Despite a troubled economy, production increased in 2010 by about 10 percent, to 1,577, and the tax dropped to $1,300. Economic realities caught up with discretionary spending for 2011 model year, and ZR1 production dropped by almost half, to 806 units. Suggested retail price had crept up to $110,750, and a new regular production option PBC allowed ZR1 (or Z06) buyers to help assemble their own engine at Chevrolet's Wixom, Michigan, plant. Only 16 buyers took advantage of this $5,800 experience.

The economy slammed ZR1 production again for 2012, reducing assembly to just 404 cars. The price climbed incrementally, to $112,500, and fuel economy improved by 1 mile-per-gallon when engineers recalibrated transmission gear ratios for 5th and 6th. As a result, the gas-guzzler tax dropped to $1,000. Michelin Pilot Sport Cup tires were an option, along with lighter wheels, a close-ratio transmission, and a full-width rear spoiler in black, all inspired by Corvette's success in the American Le Mans series of endurance races. Chevrolet still offered the engine-build experience, though only 12 buyers took advantage of the opportunity.

Aside from its phenomenal top speed and exceptional acceleration, the ZR1 models were known for excellent handling, and their chassis and wide tires (285/30R-19 up front and 335/25R-20 at the rear) gave the car skidpad lateral acceleration of 1.15G. Yet the 3,414-pound car was manageable and even docile as a daily driver, albeit one with extraordinary capabilities.

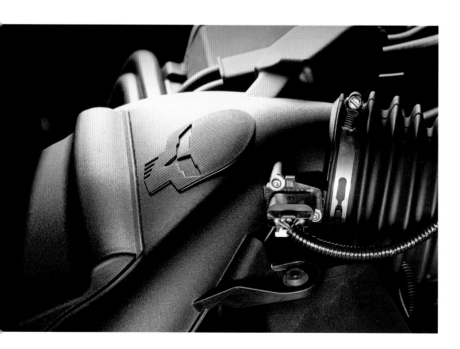

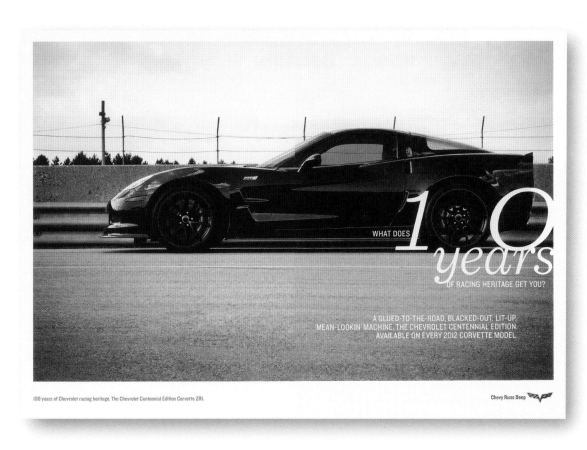

WHAT DOES 100 years OF RACING HERITAGE GET YOU?

A GLUED-TO-THE-ROAD, BLACKED-OUT, LIT-UP, MEAN-LOOKIN' MACHINE. THE CHEVROLET CENTENNIAL EDITION. AVAILABLE ON EVERY 2012 CORVETTE MODEL.

100 years of Chevrolet racing heritage. The Chevrolet Centennial Edition Corvette ZR1.

Chevy Runs Deep

22

2014
C7 STINGRAY
Coupe

As has been the case since 1953, the introduction of the seventh-generation Corvette proved to be one of the American auto industry's most anxiously awaited launches. Chevrolet division clamped NSA-type security onto the project for nearly all of its design and development time. Very few spy photos appeared until Chevrolet was ready to tease and tantalize potential buyers. One of the first surprises was Chevrolet's reactivation of the long-lived and much-loved Stingray name, now as one word.

ENGINEERS ADOPTED the aluminum chassis technology of previous generation C6 model ZR1 and Z06 performance editions. However a significant redesign and re-engineering pulled 100 pounds of weight off the previous frame while giving it 50 percent more stiffness for better ride and road holding.

For the C7's engine, Chevy powerplant engineers and product planners resurrected an earlier code for a previous "small block" high performer, the LT1. In the newest 6.2-liter version—348 cubic inches—output rose to 455 horsepower, achieved by incorporating direct fuel injection and continuously variable valve timing. A computerized cylinder deactivation feature and a new seven-speed manual gearbox helped the car reach 17 mile-per-gallon city fuel economy and 29 mile-per-gallon frugality on the highway. Owners reported 7th-gear deactivated-cylinder cruises at closer above 35 mpg. In another change, Chevrolet assembled these

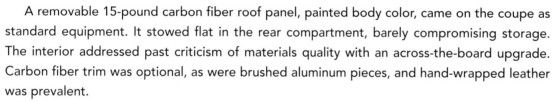

A removable 15-pound carbon fiber roof panel, painted body color, came on the coupe as standard equipment. It stowed flat in the rear compartment, barely compromising storage. The interior addressed past criticism of materials quality with an across-the-board upgrade. Carbon fiber trim was optional, as were brushed aluminum pieces, and hand-wrapped leather was prevalent.

Chevrolet debuted the C7 Stingray at the North American International Auto Show in Detroit in January 2013. But it was many months before coupes found their way to the road. Corvette introduced the base coupe at $51,995, and the convertible arrived a few months later at $56,995. Various Z-coded models arrived through 2014 calendar year. With all the new technology—and much-welcomed new seats—the 2014 models were only $1,420 more expensive than the 2013 base coupe and convertibles.

Electronics were a by-word of modern automobiles, and the C7 Stingray operated with electronic power steering, an electronic parking brake, a pair of eight-inch high-definition display screens, and even an electronic limited slip differential on the rear transaxle on the performance Z51 models. (This system was part of what helped the C7 reach a long-held goal of 50/50 weight balance between front and rear.)

Both of the project chiefs on the C7—Tadge Juechter for engineering and Tom Peters on design and styling—were Corvette veterans, each having held the same roles on the previous C6 models. While some voices had criticized the C6 as only an evolution from the C5, perhaps more a C5.5 than a whole new car, the C7 distinctively marked its territory with its edgy, aggressive styling and its up-to-the-instant engineering and performance.

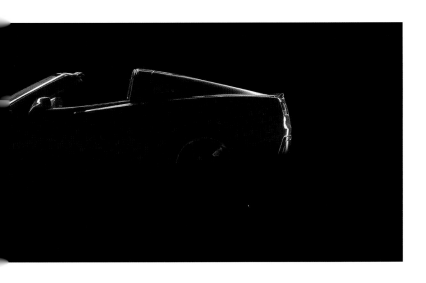

PHOTOGRAPHER'S NOTES

Car photographers have a number of techniques we can use to "light" the car. I probably am best known as an "available light" shooter. I spend most of a day finding a suitable location for an automobile I need for one of my books. Then, three or four hours before dark, the owner and I go to this spot for me to photograph it. However, with the increasing number of books featuring automobiles shot in a studio and treating them as sculpture, my editor suggested the time had

1

For an earlier project titled *Top Muscle*, Dave introduced me to the CamRanger. This electronic device lets a photographer operate his modern-day auto-everything Nikon/Canon/Otherwise equipment by remote control. Dave fires his using his iPhone. I wanted bigger images, so I set up mine to run through my iPad, which I mounted on a lightweight tripod. CamRanger (http://www.camranger.com) establishes its own Wi-Fi network connecting your iPhone or iPad to your intelligent camera. You can adjust aperture, shutter time, and even wirelessly shift focus on auto-focus lenses. The benefit of this is you can do this light-painting process without an assistant to "push the button." With my iPad, I saw quickly whether I'd succeeded or failed with the most recent exposure. I shoot RAW, but the CamRanger works most efficiently with small jpegs so I reset my Nikon D800 to do both.

This technique is different from traditional automotive studio photography. In that approach (also in a dark space), the photographer uses a light box suspended from the ceiling or supported by sturdy light stands at each corner. Some shooters used commercially available systems, from Chimera for example (http://www.chimeralighting.com), that are 20 feet long. Others have had lights made-to-order and stretch more than twice that length. The advantage to the greater length

Raw materials: Car, space, and controllable light. Inside a building, you must have nearly absolute dark to avoid retouching away reflections and stray lights. It's the same at night because streetlights and building security lamps will add time to Photoshop retouching efforts.

2

My first pass went high overhead, along the fender ridgeline, using the reflector light. This laid down the outline of the car, which I filled in with light from additional passes. On this Buick I did this pass several times each with the work light and again with the soft box before choosing this single pass as the start point.

This pass with the soft box overhead and aimed down onto the car, but on the far side of the car, put color on the front hood and into the interior, and added a soft reflection into the windshield and rear quarter of the car. As with the previous shot, this was one of nearly a dozen passes with the lights to get reflections where I wanted them.

This pass put the soft box about chest height, aimed at the car so the driver's side windows picked up reflection. With highly reflective surfaces, remember that angle of incidence equals angle of reflection, so think about where your light must strike the car in order to reach your lens.

is very soft elegant light that runs past the extreme ends of the car, no matter how long it is. The 20-foot boxes produce light that falls off more abruptly. The illumination source inside these large boxes is electronic strobe, usually 2,000 or 2,400 watt-second units, generally spaced about every four feet to provide even light. A 20-foot soft box might house 10 strobe heads and the cables connecting them to power packs. Those 40-foot units will double that investment. It's the effect of these 40-foot long fixtures that light painting can imitate because with the softbox or reflector-light, you can start and finish your light pass a few feet past the end of the car.

Don't shine the light in the same place every time you pass the car. Make a pass with the light at ankle height, knee height, waist height, chest height, head height, overhead. Try letting it rise and fall with the fender or roof contours. Then change from the soft box to the reflector light. Do it all over again. Every pass.

On my first light-paint book project, I experimented with LED fixtures. They are a very interesting light source, but most of the LED "soft boxes" are made up of 48 or even 400 individual LED bulbs. Many automobiles worth shooting have paint like a mirror, so every one of those LED bulbs leaves 48 or 400 streaky highlight reflections. LEDs, I learned, work best for any area lacking mirror-finished paint such as interiors and engine compartments without chrome.

So if no LEDs, then what? Go to http://www.BandH.com and order their 12-inch Impact photoflood reflector. This brushed aluminum "bowl" makes a beautiful light with a 75-watt bulb in it.

Then look for a 24x32-inch white soft box. These manageable dimensions allow you easily and safely to maneuver it around, along, and over the car you're shooting. You might visit your nearest professional photo equipment supplier to inspect these light sources. Find a box that seals up light tightly at the rear. Manufacturers are inconsistent. Some Chimera boxes fully envelop the rear of the light very effectively, blocking most of the extraneous light. Other styles of the same size have gaps large enough to put your hand through, and this will leave unwanted light trails through your shot. This isn't a design flaw, merely the reality that very few photographers position their softboxes directly in front of the lens where light out the back will spoil the shot. (If your photo supplier has opened and let you examine a number of boxes, you should buy the one you like best right then and there. This not only supports your supplier but also ensures that you have it because manufacturers change designs and their own outside suppliers without notice.) Securely mount a 200-watt bulb inside it that so it doesn't touch the diffusion cloth and burn a hole. Resist the temptation to order silver soft boxes or zebra-striped ones. I wanted to experiment and I paid the price when it came time to assemble these images in Photoshop. I tried and failed with all kinds of bad ideas while doing my first light-paint shoot. Thirty muscle cars shot over about 20 calendar days provided abundant opportunity to make serious errors. However, this pace represented just about the right amount of repetition to begin to understand how this process works. I nearly had this shooting technique dialed in as I drove away from these collections. And that helped considerably when it came time to light-paint Corvettes for this book some months later. But "painting" the car with light is only the beginning. This was the easy part.

I've used Adobe Photoshop for years and made primary adjustments in color balance, contrast, shadow, and highlight preservation. As a light-painter, I did all those and much, much more.

The problem at that point was that even though I saw each light pass come up on the iPad screen, I had no idea whether I really had succeeded or failed at getting something that was going to help me "assemble" a car. That became clear when I got home and began to work with what I'd shot. For that first book, out of 30 cars, out of six or seven or eight views of each car, I seldom had enough passes. Some views were so bad they are not in this book. Others are simply miracles of luck and preparation.

Dave Wendt warned me, "Shoot and keep shooting. Be sure you have enough passes." I'll add: when you believe you are done, start all over again and shoot more. This is not an obsessive-compulsive speaking but a recommendation—and experience—from one who did not follow advice. I followed that advice more faithfully on this project. But still I forgot to light important edges and surfaces of the cars.

For my first book, I established a production goal of shooting two complete cars per 10- or 11-hour day, five days a week. This meant side profile view, 3/4 front, 3/4 rear, an engine view or two, an interior view or two, and a detail view or two. This was too ambitious. For this Corvette project, I scheduled only a single car on any given shoot day. Even so, each Corvette required between four and six hours to shoot. By the time you are on your last views, you will have walked past the car hundreds of times with your softbox and reflector light. You will swear you have covered every angle and facet, that you have highlighted or outlined every surface or edge. Likely as not, when you get to your computer, you will swear at yourself because in your confusion, you did miss something.

I liken my earliest light-painting effort to learning to play three-dimensional chess wearing a blindfold. You can think about and visualize what you are doing, but you have no idea what it looks like—even when you see your most recent exposure on the CamRanger screen. Does that exposure—or

5

On this pass, aiming the work light away from the camera but toward the car illuminated the color without adding unwanted reflections. The light was close to the body—and dragged along the floor—to sharpen cutoff along the body "beltline." It provided a valuable highlight along that line as well. This was another case where more than a dozen passes with the two lights led me to this exposure that not only shows the car but defines its shape.

6

Passing the soft box along the front of the car filled in the grille, headlight frames, the bumper, and the license plate. Try this with the soft box and with the work light. The effects are very different. I almost always make these passes, though sometimes spill light from light passes along the side or over the upper body surface provide a more subtle fill for this area.

several of them—give you what you need to define, describe, or sculpt the car? The moment of truth arrives when you get to the computer to begin "assembling" the views and the cars. If you're not adept at Photoshop, take a course (and not just a basic one). If you already are Photoshop fluent, take a look at your computer screen. You have hundreds of choices and options available to you. Pull down every menu, examine every possible list, consider even the remotest option, and translate all that to the possible treatments you can apply to all the cars, to every view, to each layer of each view of each car.

Assembling these images is a matter of making layers, using masks, and adding one on top of the next, accumulating the passes of light to shape and color the car. You can modify the light in every layer—you are not locked into using each exposure as shot. If you're not Photoshop-fluent—and I still am far from it—this will be another challenge. Seek help among your fellow photographers who are experienced Photoshop practitioners. Figure you'll spend nearly two hours in Photoshop for every hour you spent shooting.

The best of my images in this book don't come close to what Dave or others of the finest light-painters can do. But I really love to shoot Corvettes because of their lines and forms. This became a great opportunity to look at and photograph the cars differently.

Final exposure took place with room lights off, and neither work light nor soft box lit. With an open shutter, I flashed the parking lights on and off so that they registered without burning out the facets in their lenses. Headlights, taillights, and marker lights on a car shot in the dark work better on some cars than others. Personal taste and experimentation will dictate what looks best.

RIGHT: Final composite.

INDEX